There are no rules with this sketchbook. Just images that prompt your imagination and inspire you to express whatever you want, in whatever format you want.

Feel like writing a story to match each image?
Go for it.

Sketching or doodling backdrops on each page?
Go for that as well.

How about collaging some magazine cutouts on top – or cutting the pages out and sticking them somewhere else??
GO FOT IT!

You get the idea.

How you use this book is up to you!

Be Free!

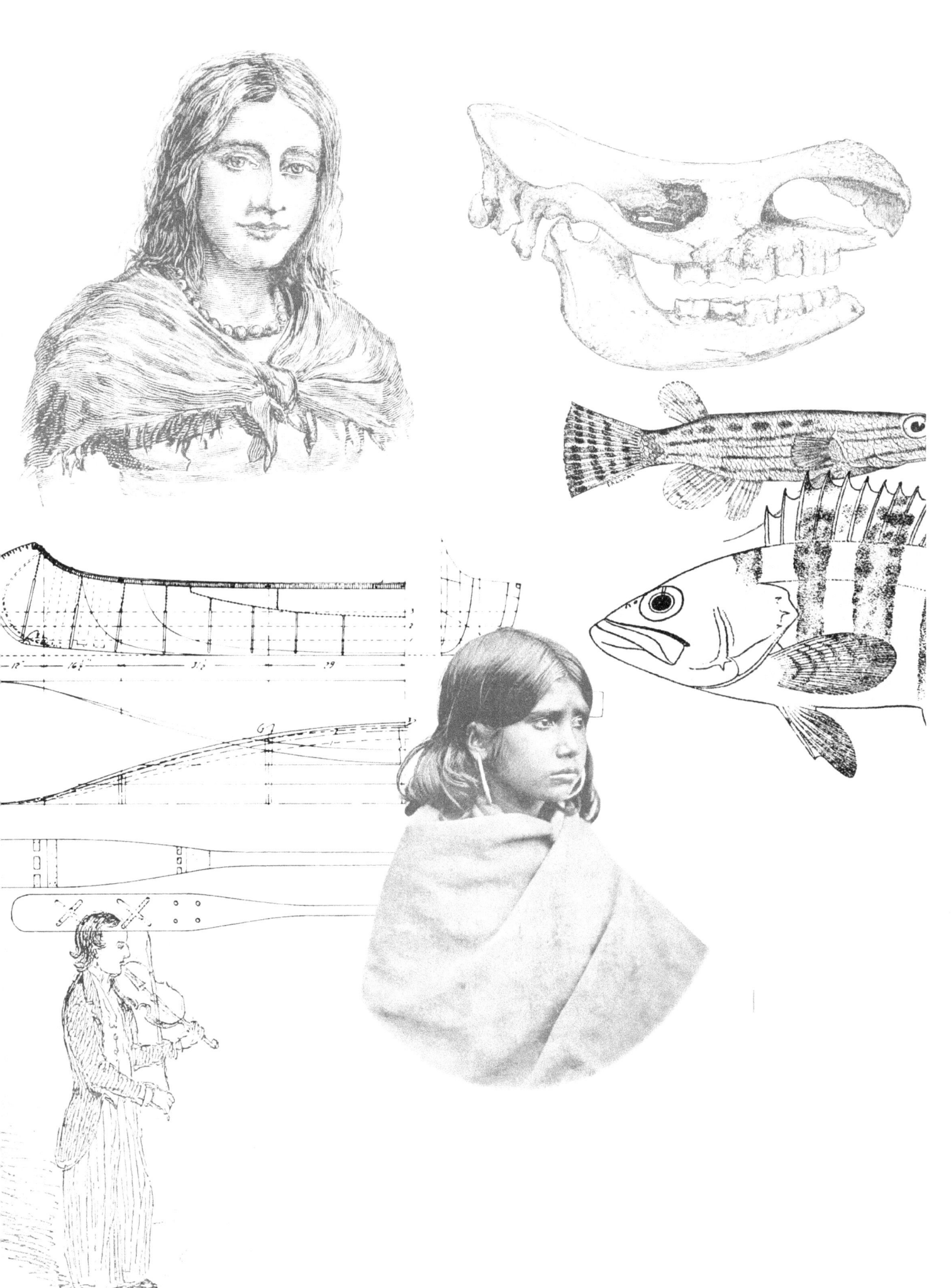

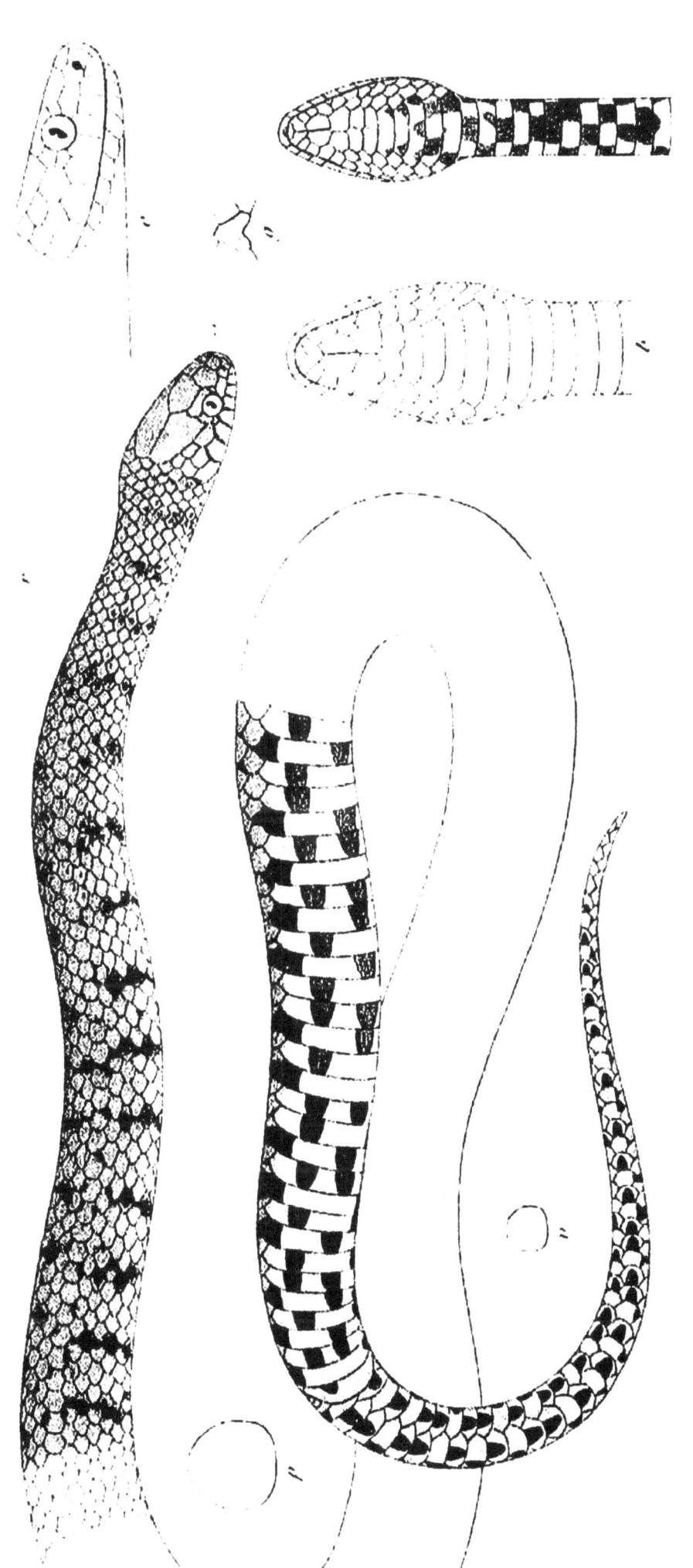

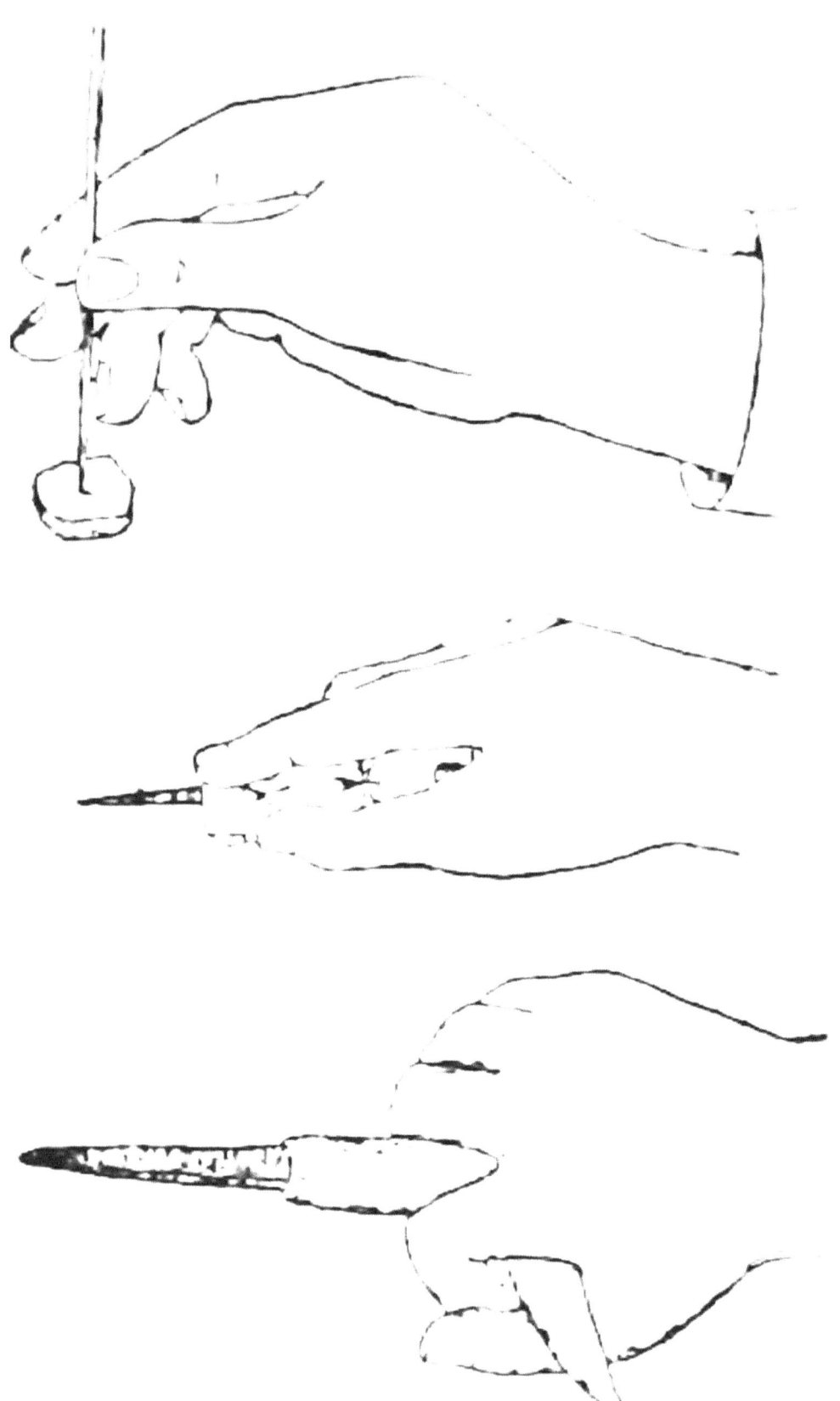

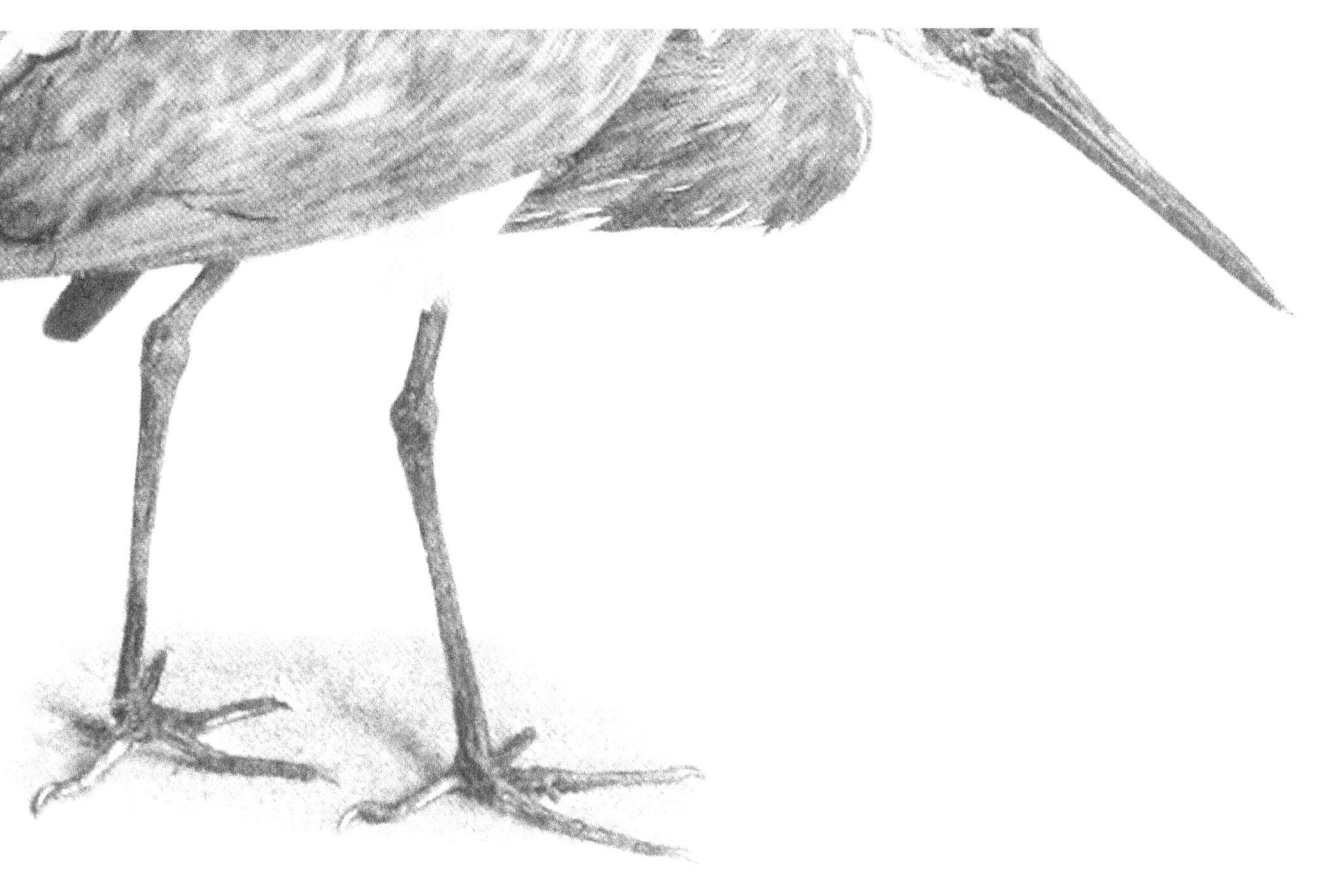

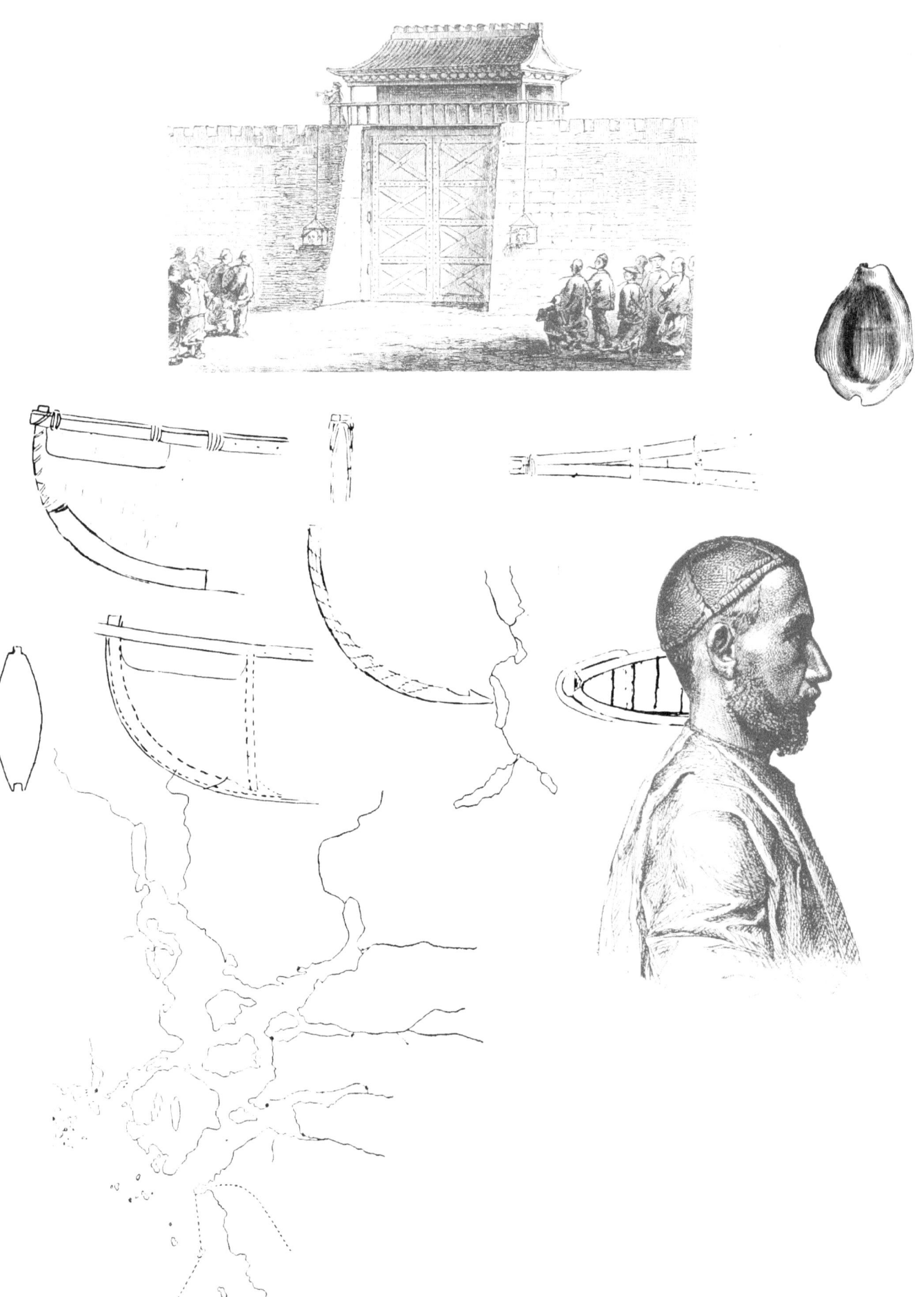

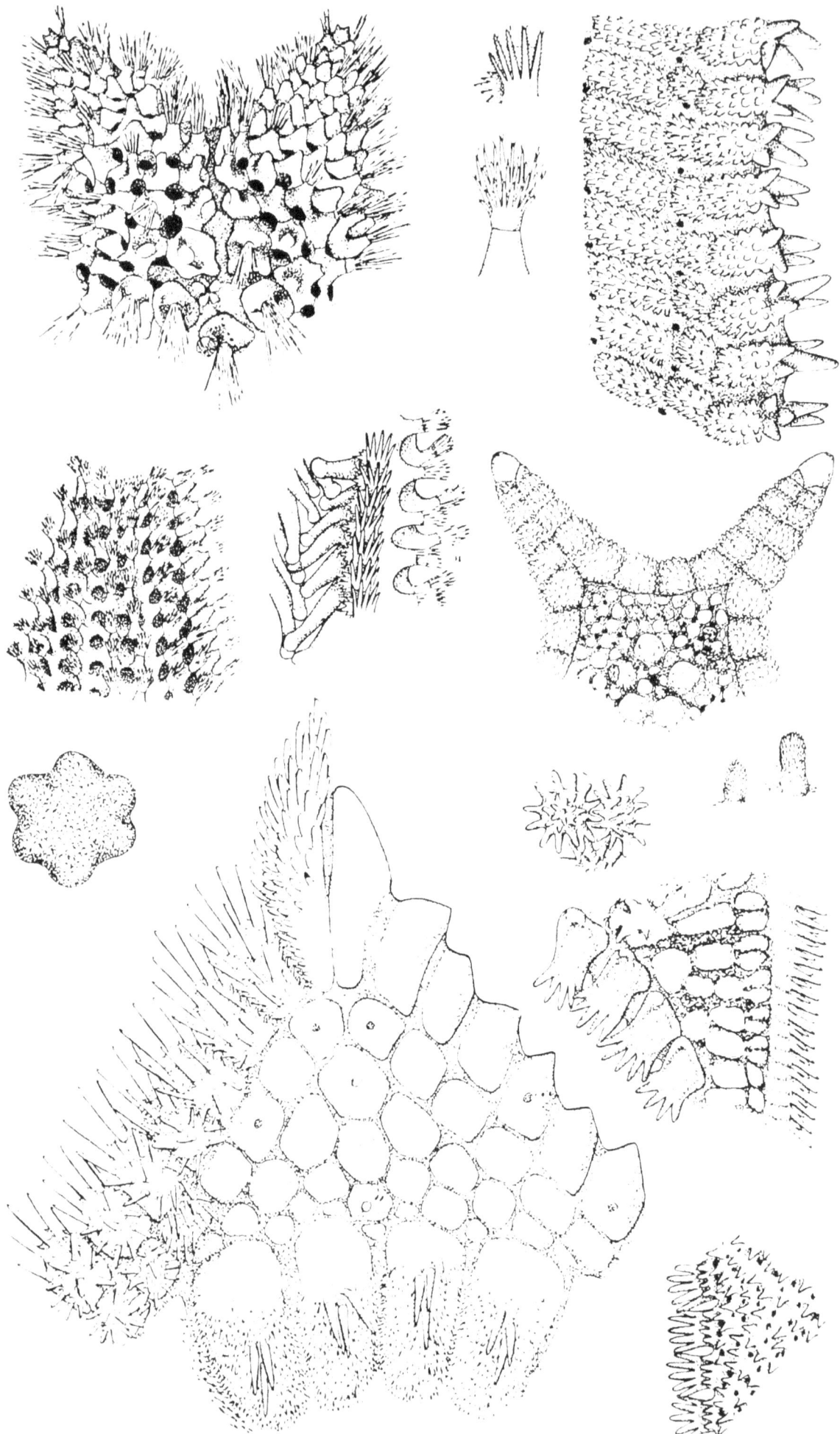

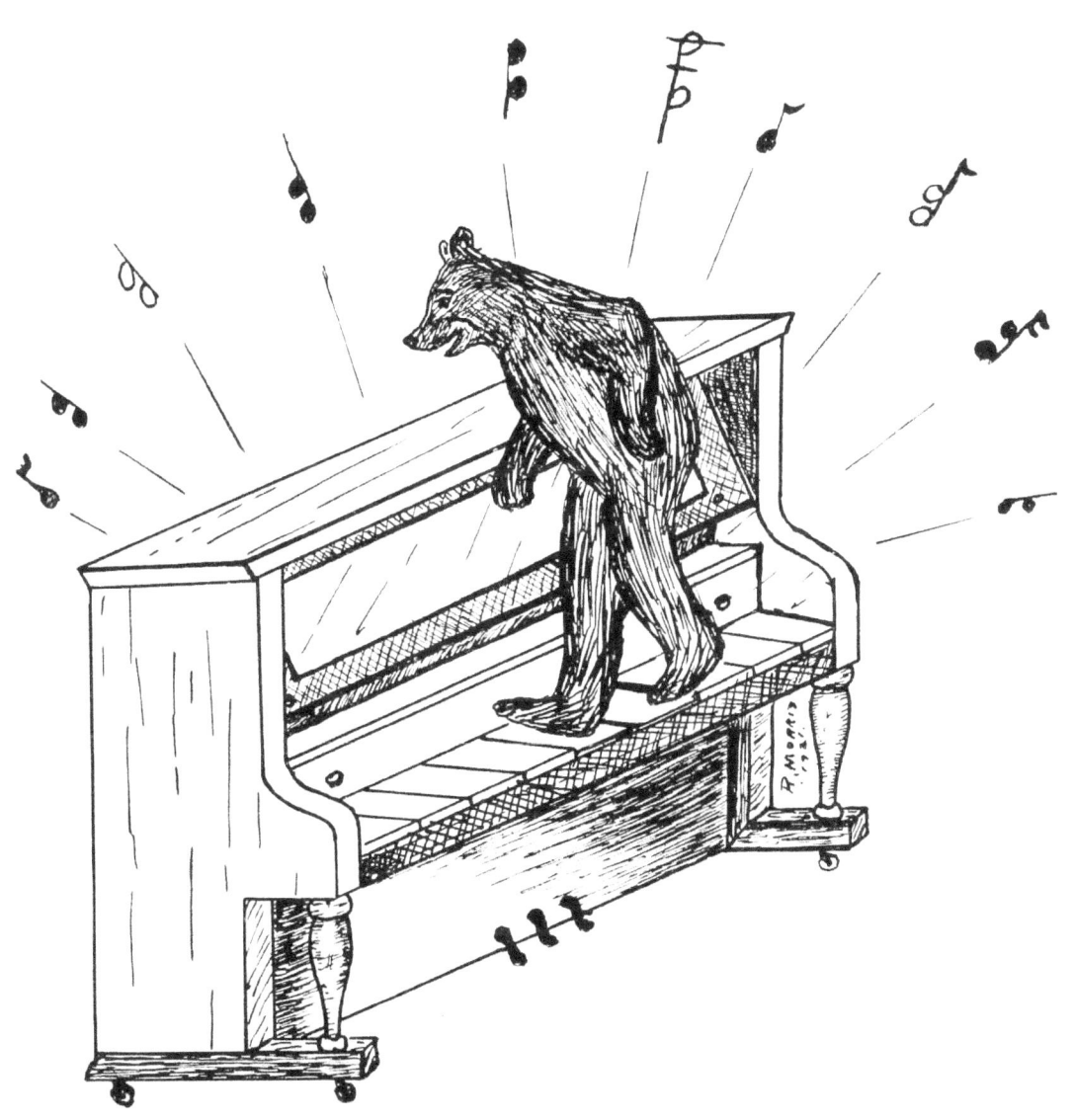

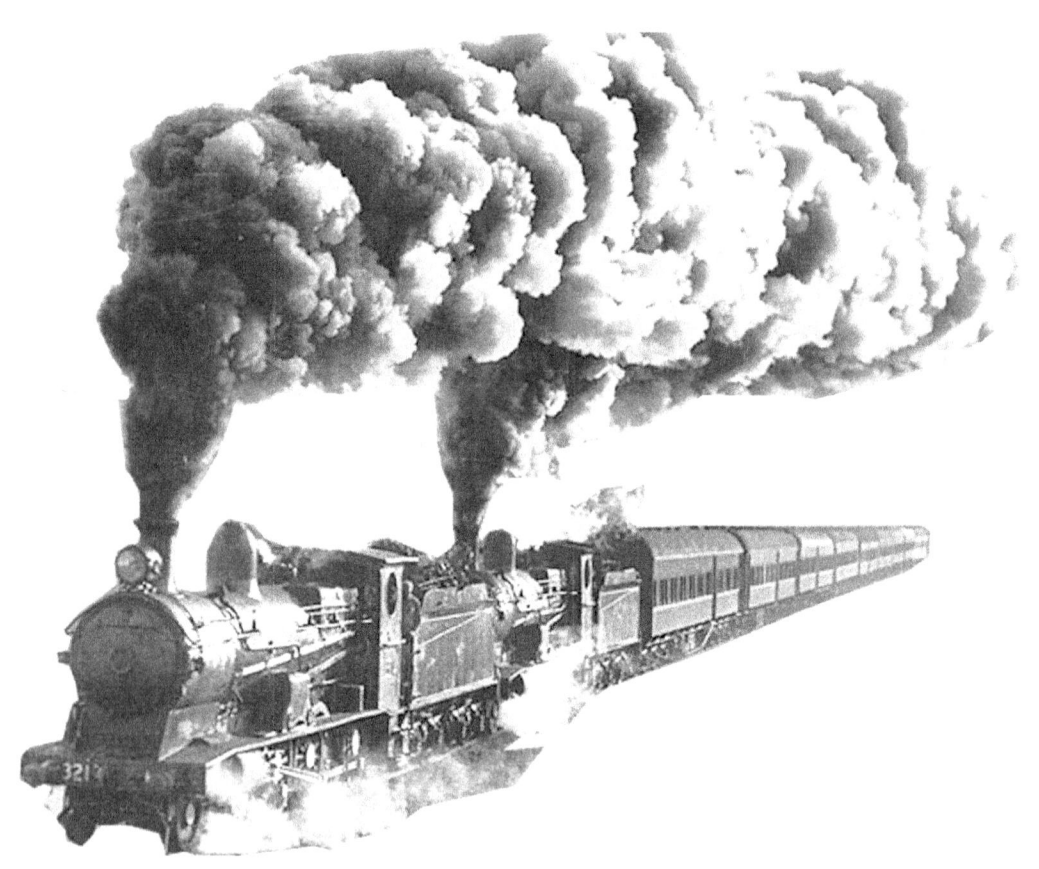

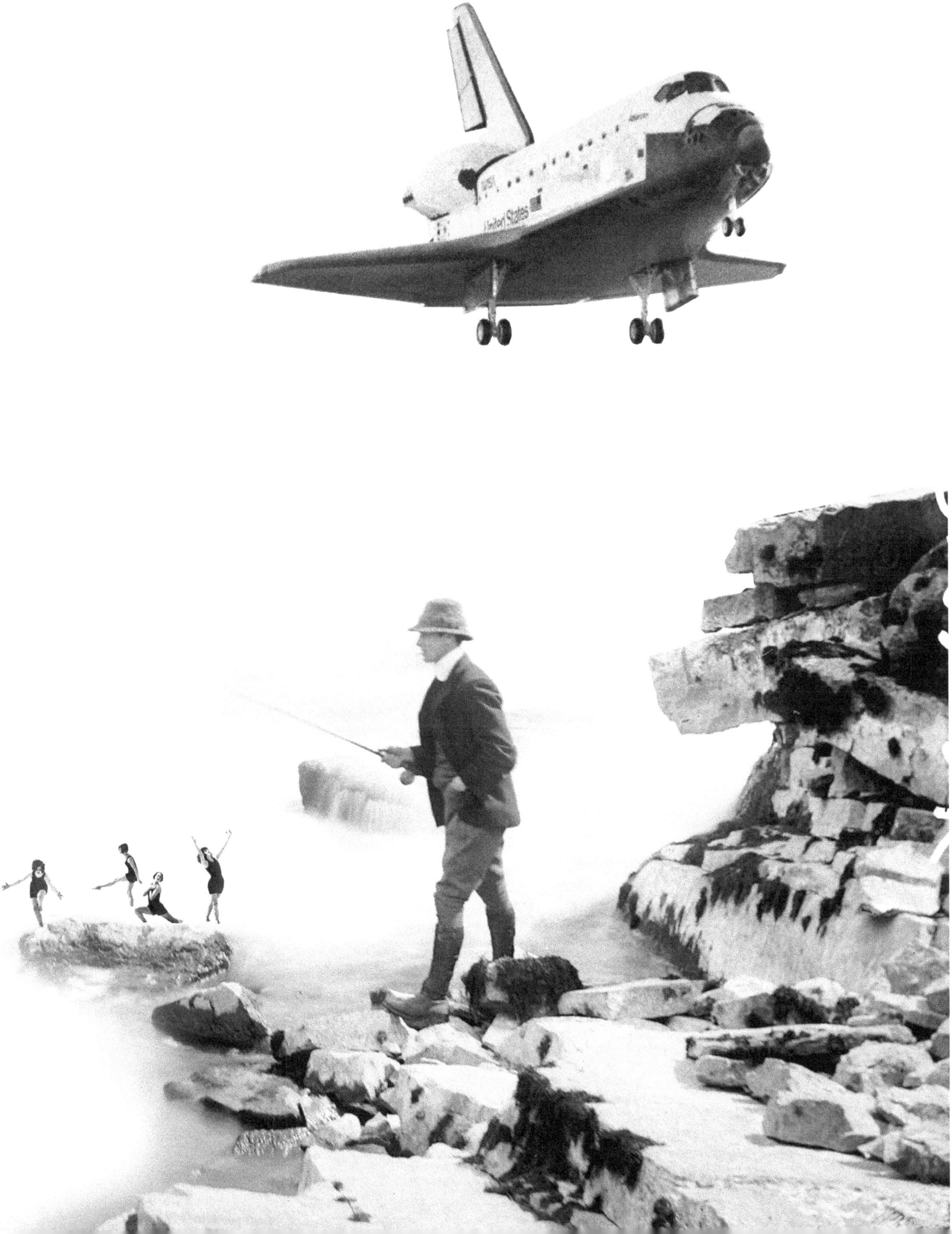

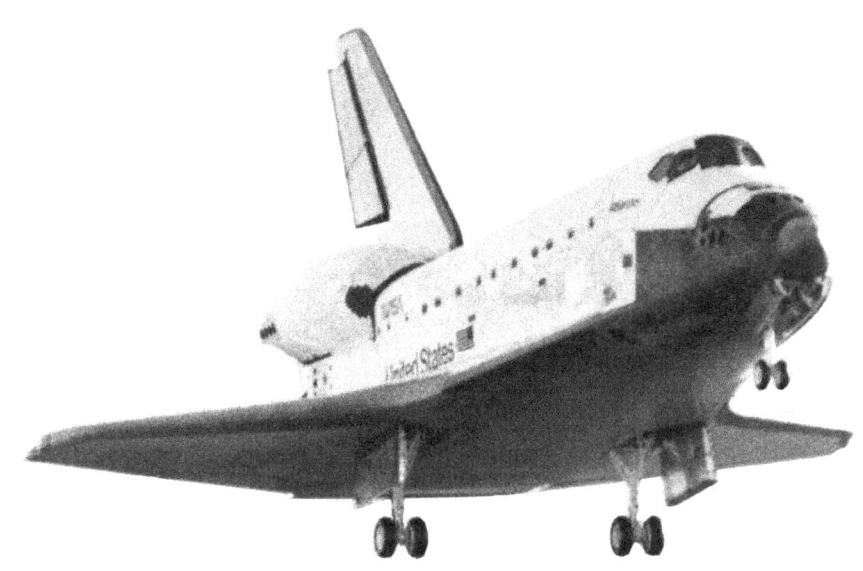

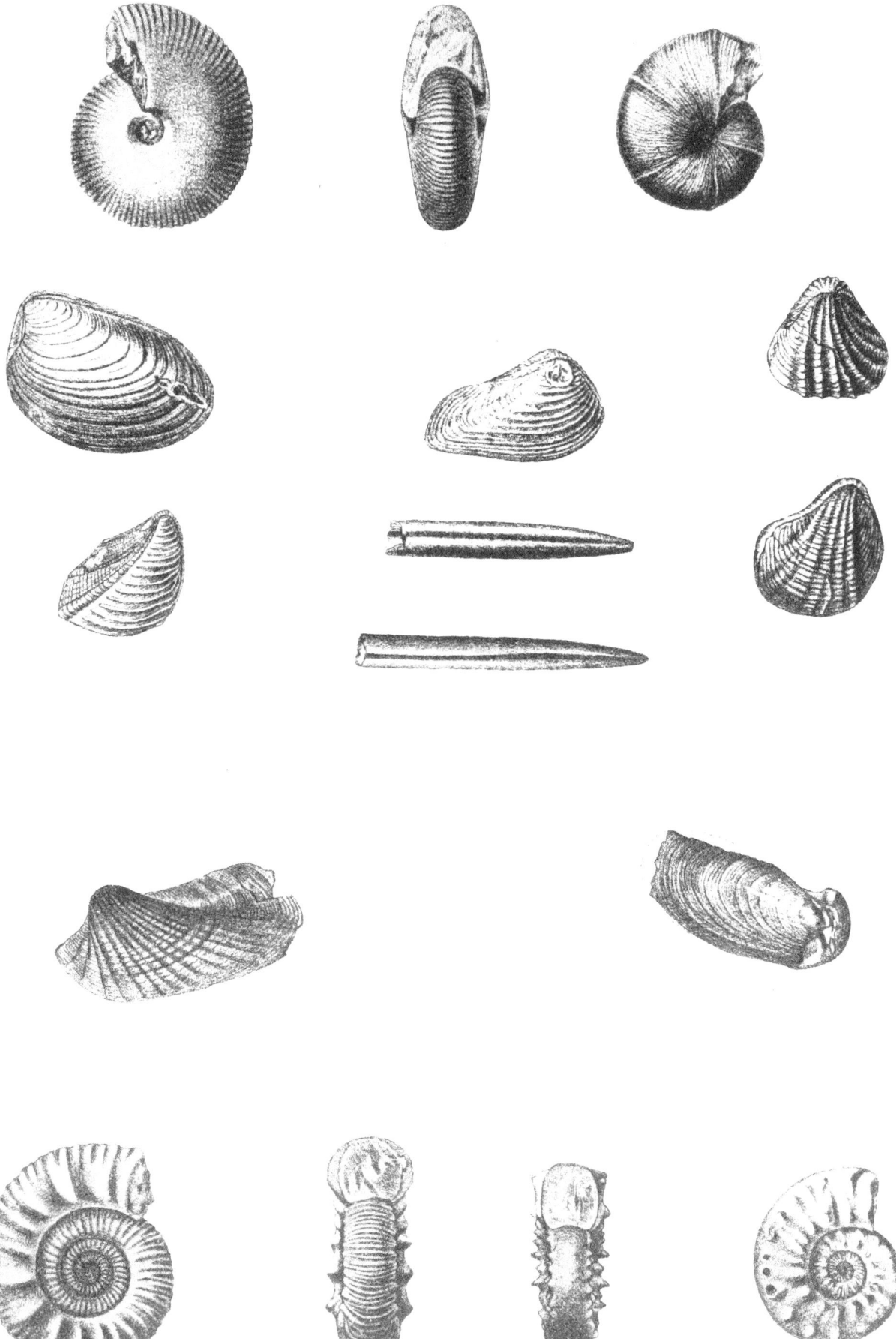

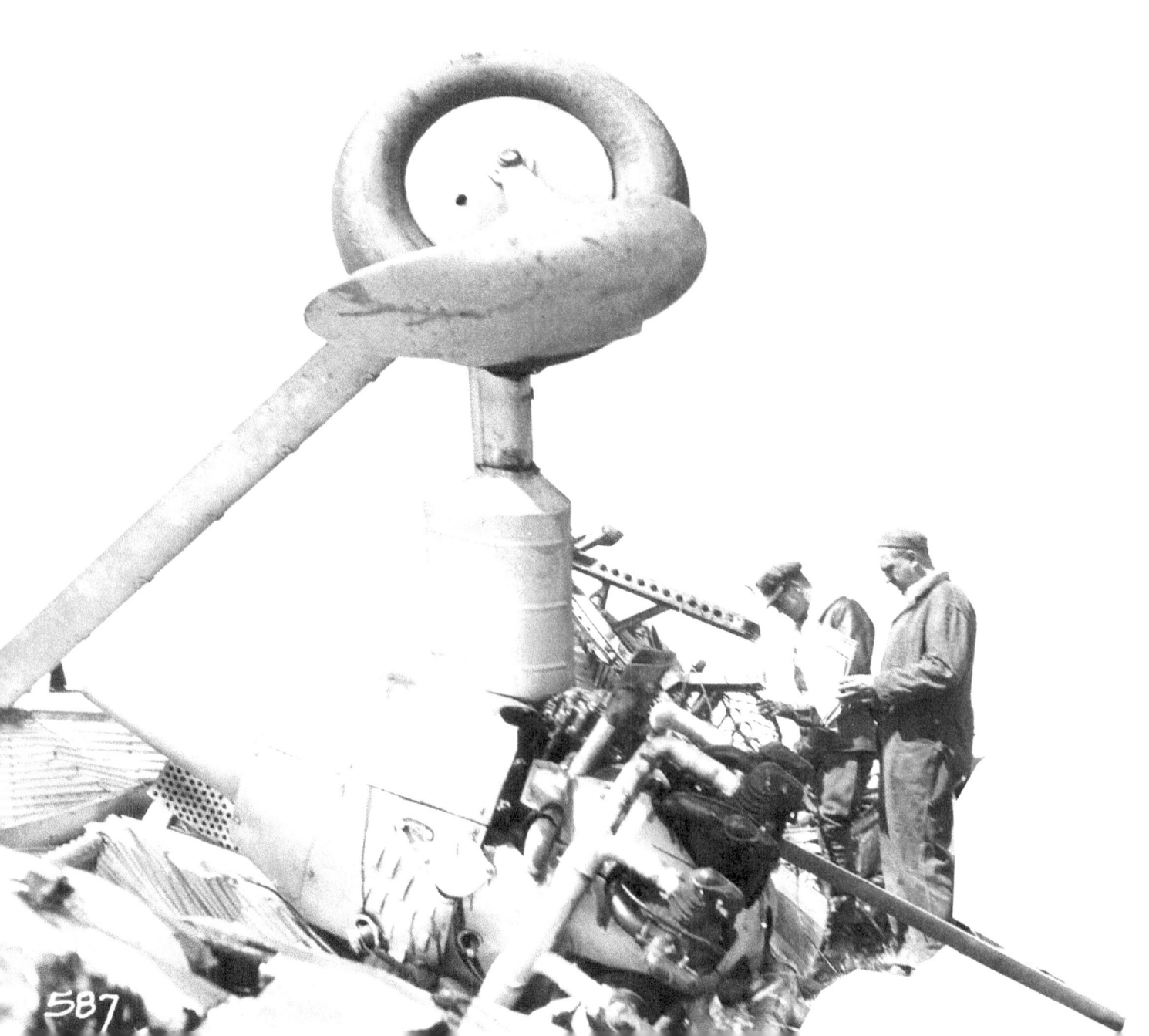

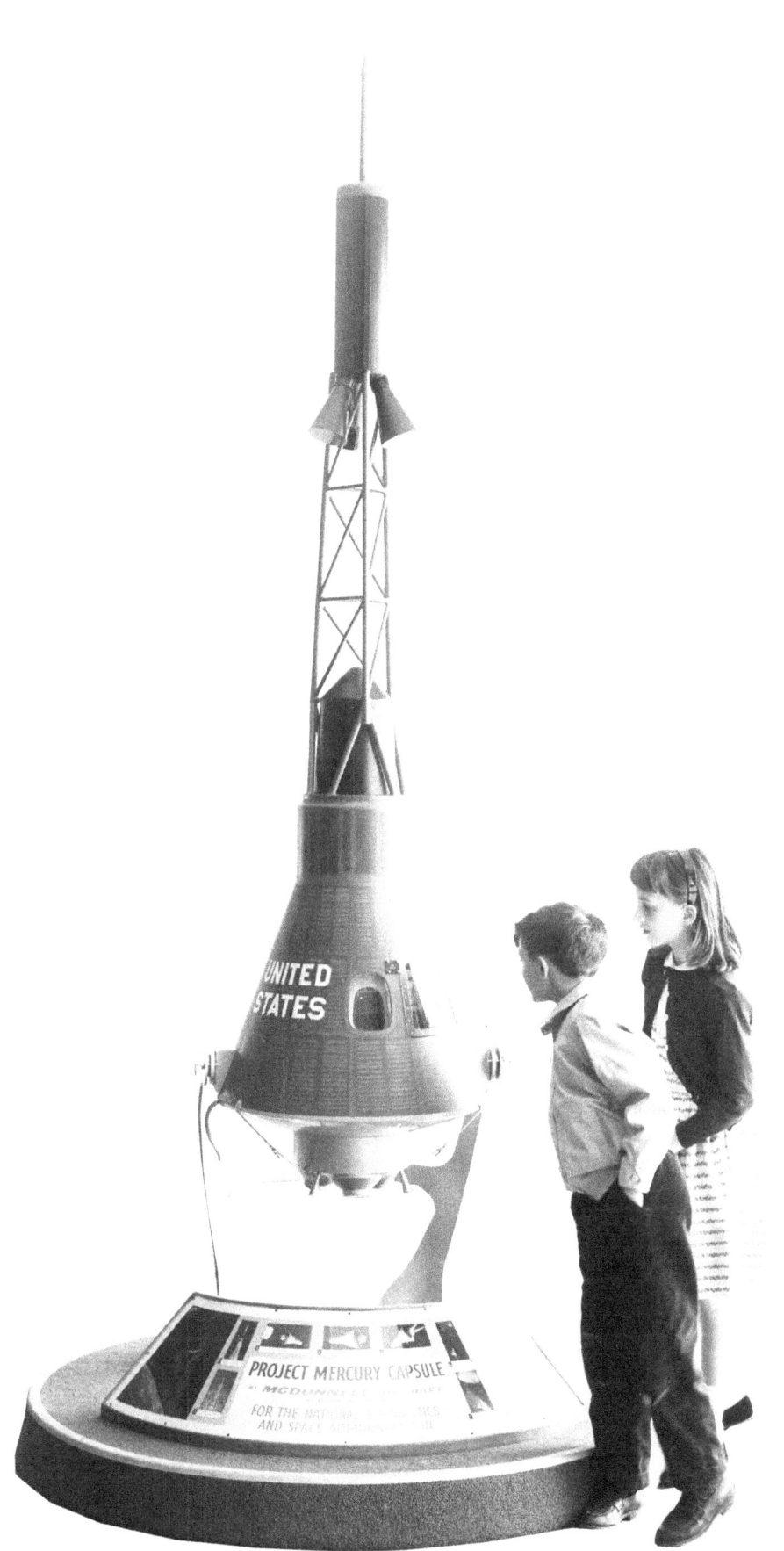

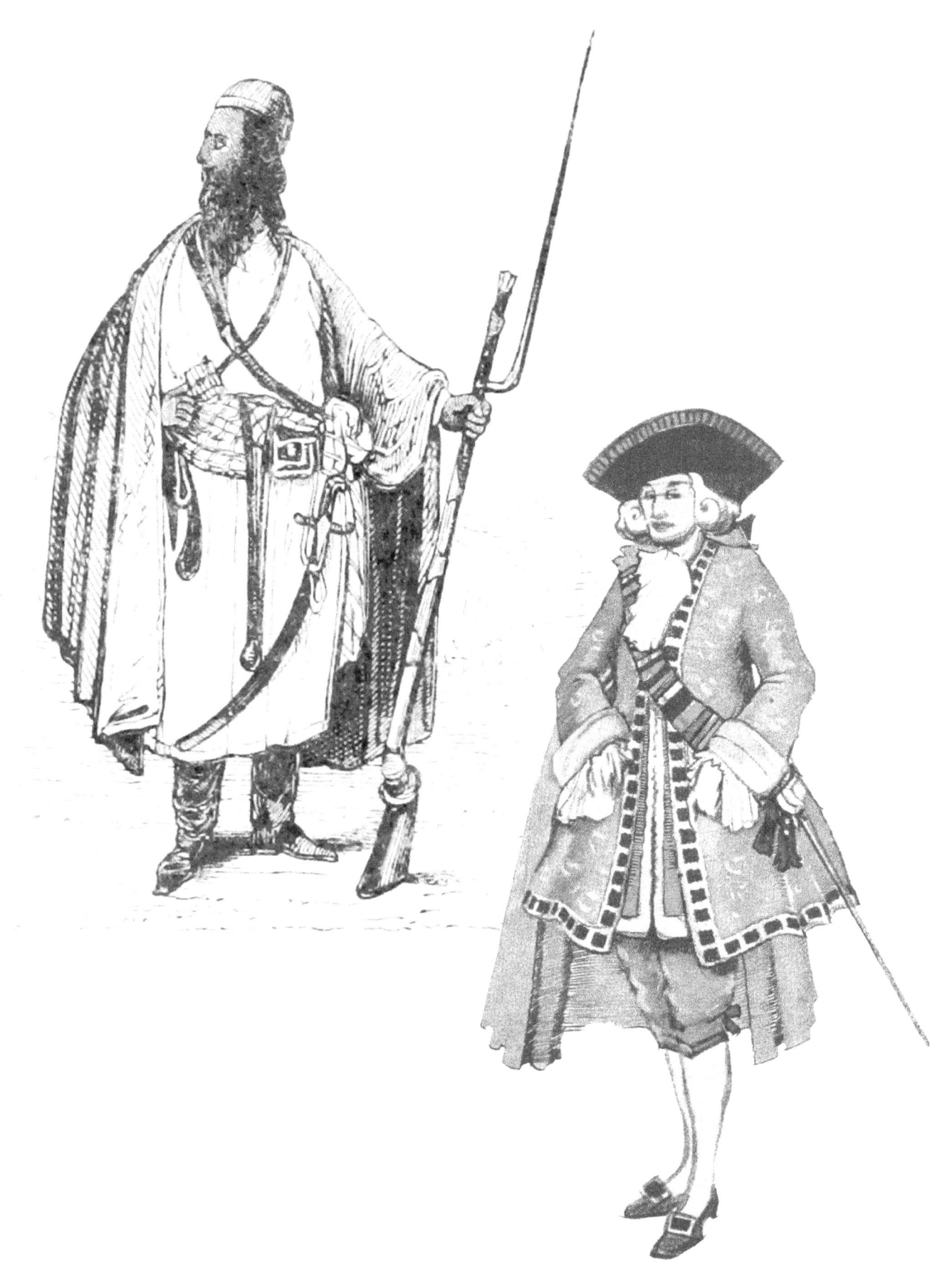

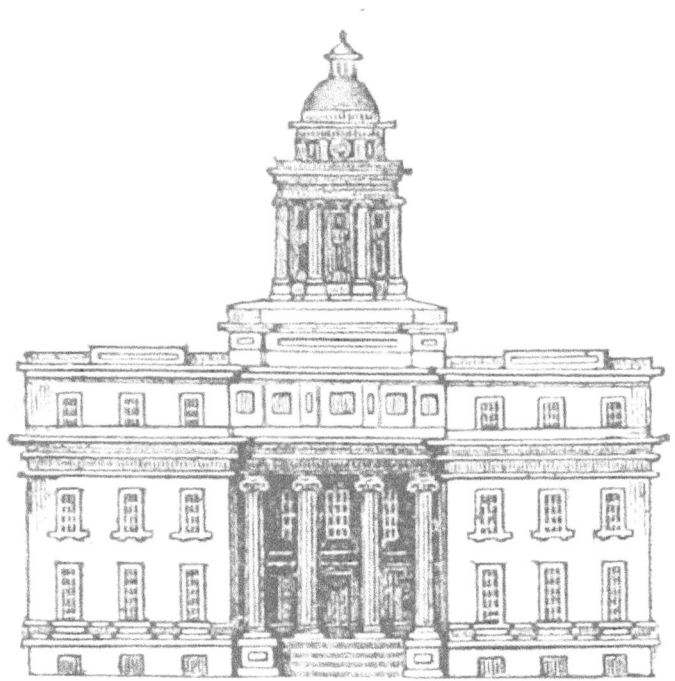

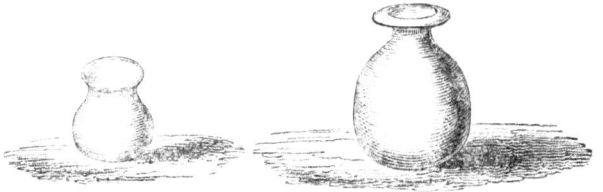

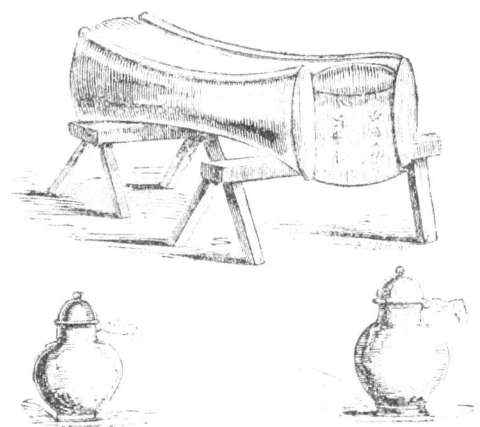

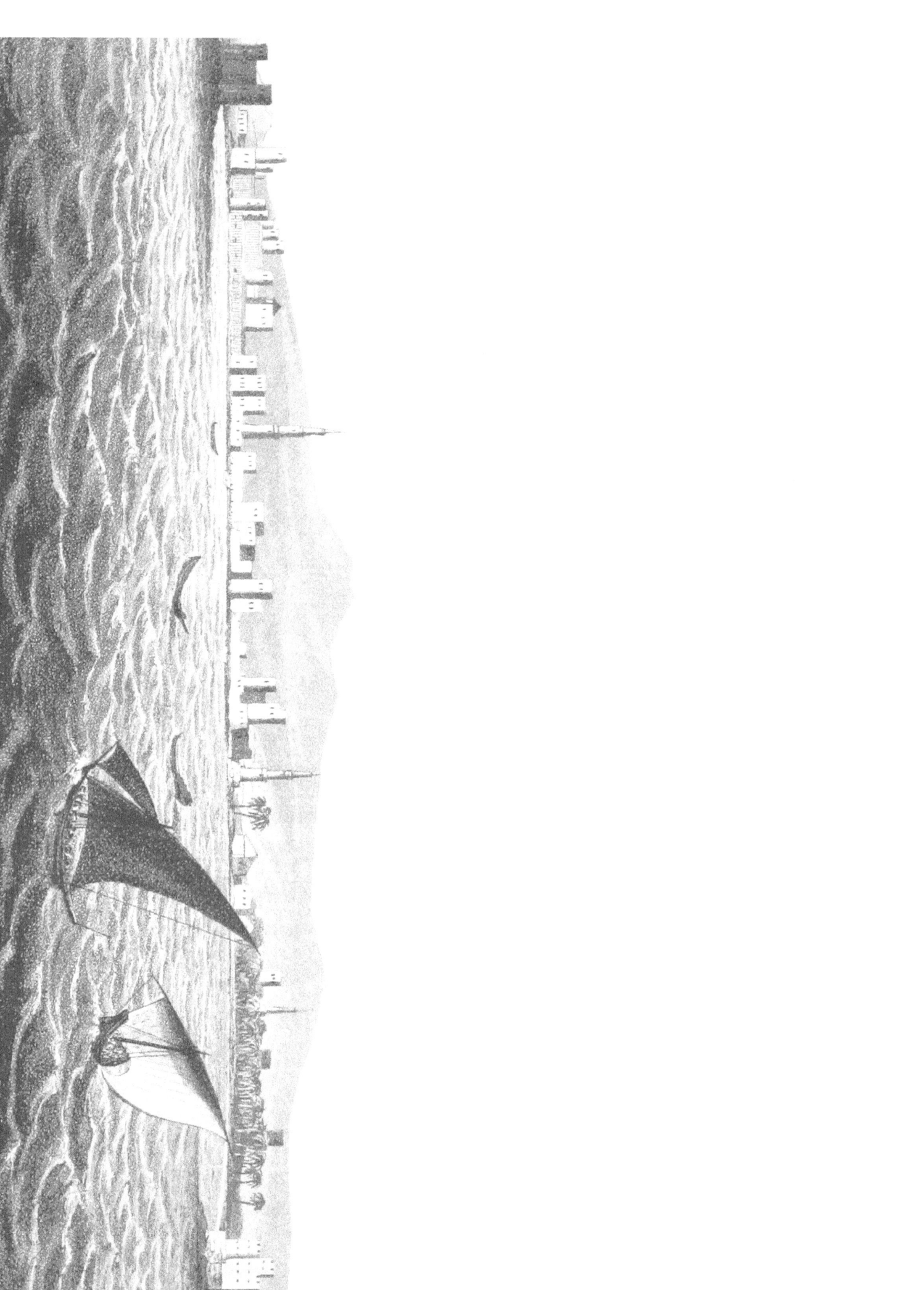

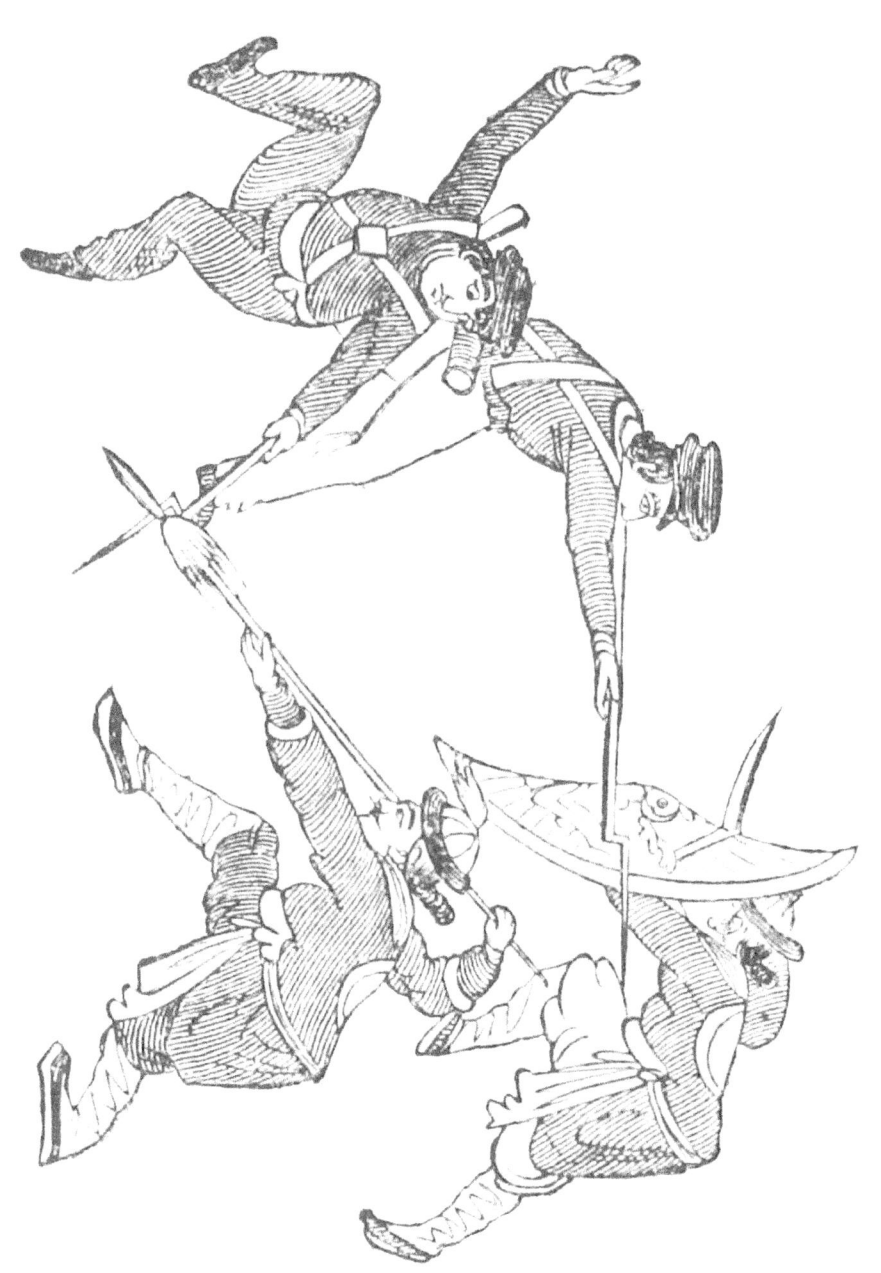

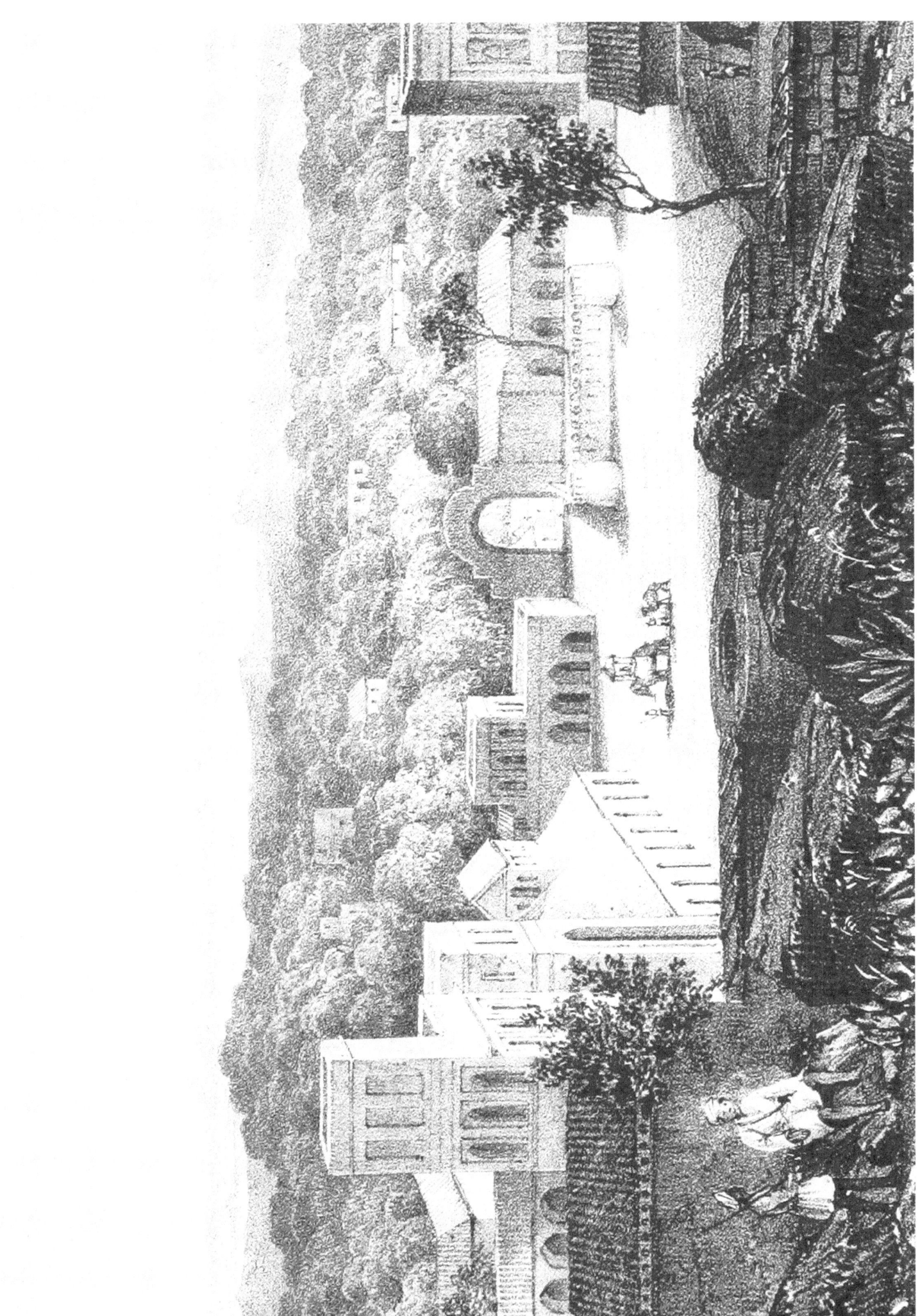

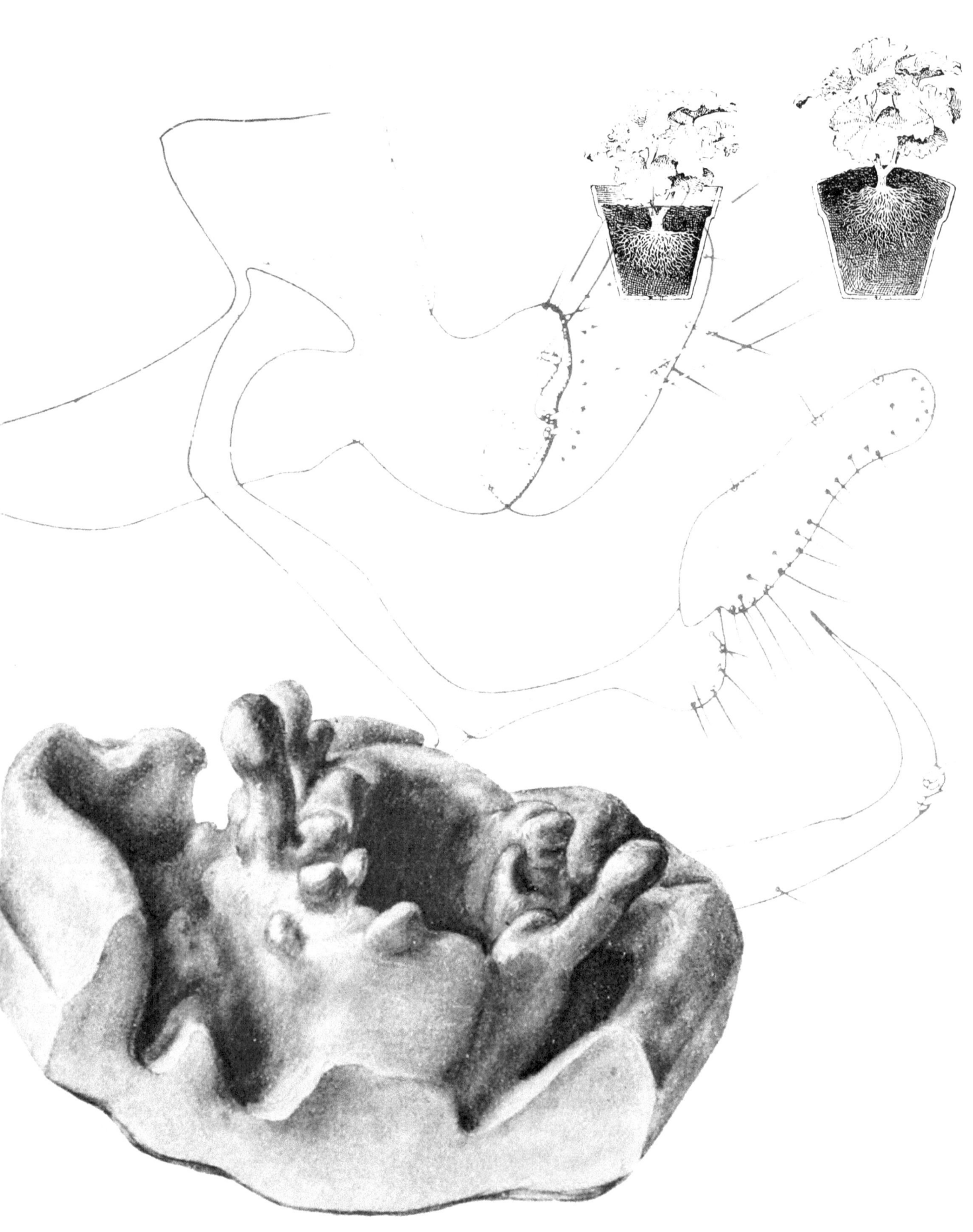

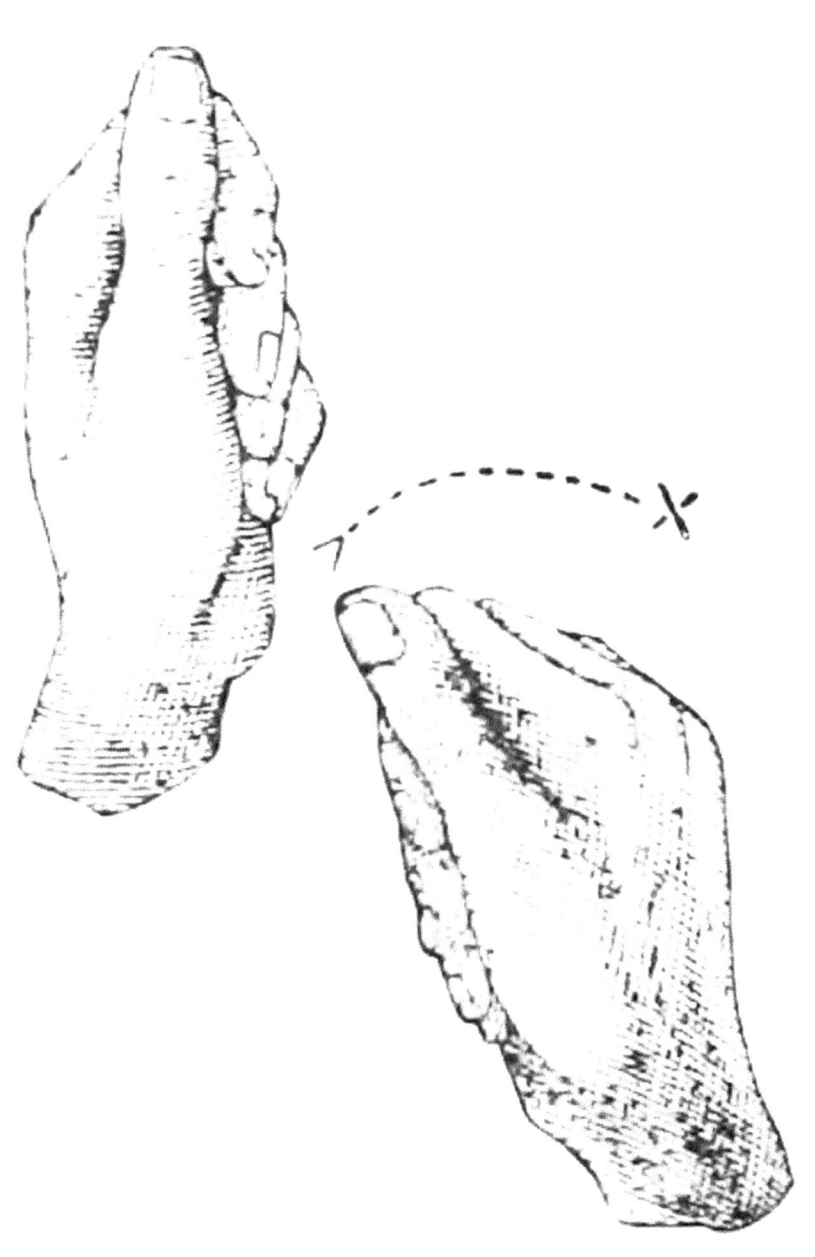

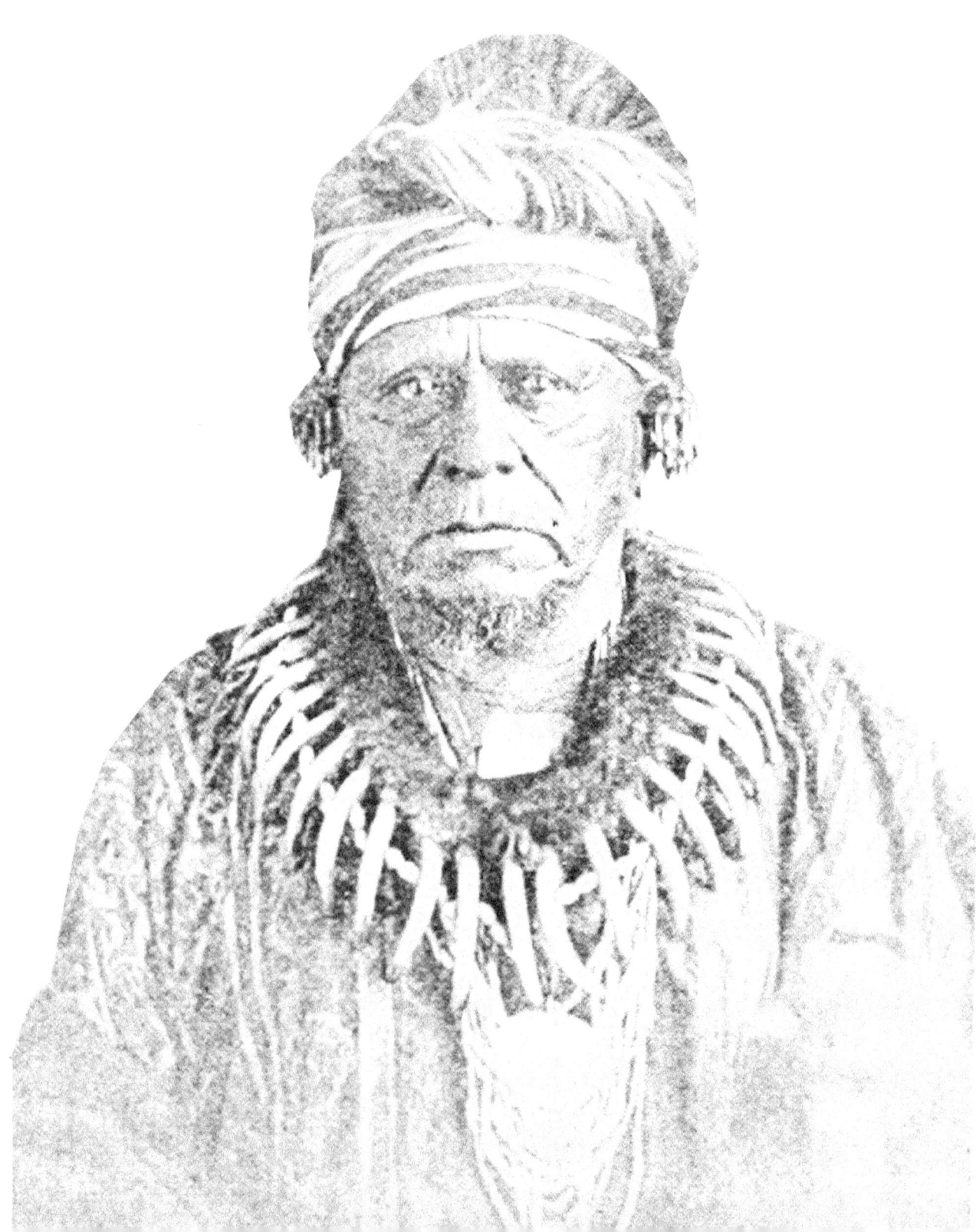

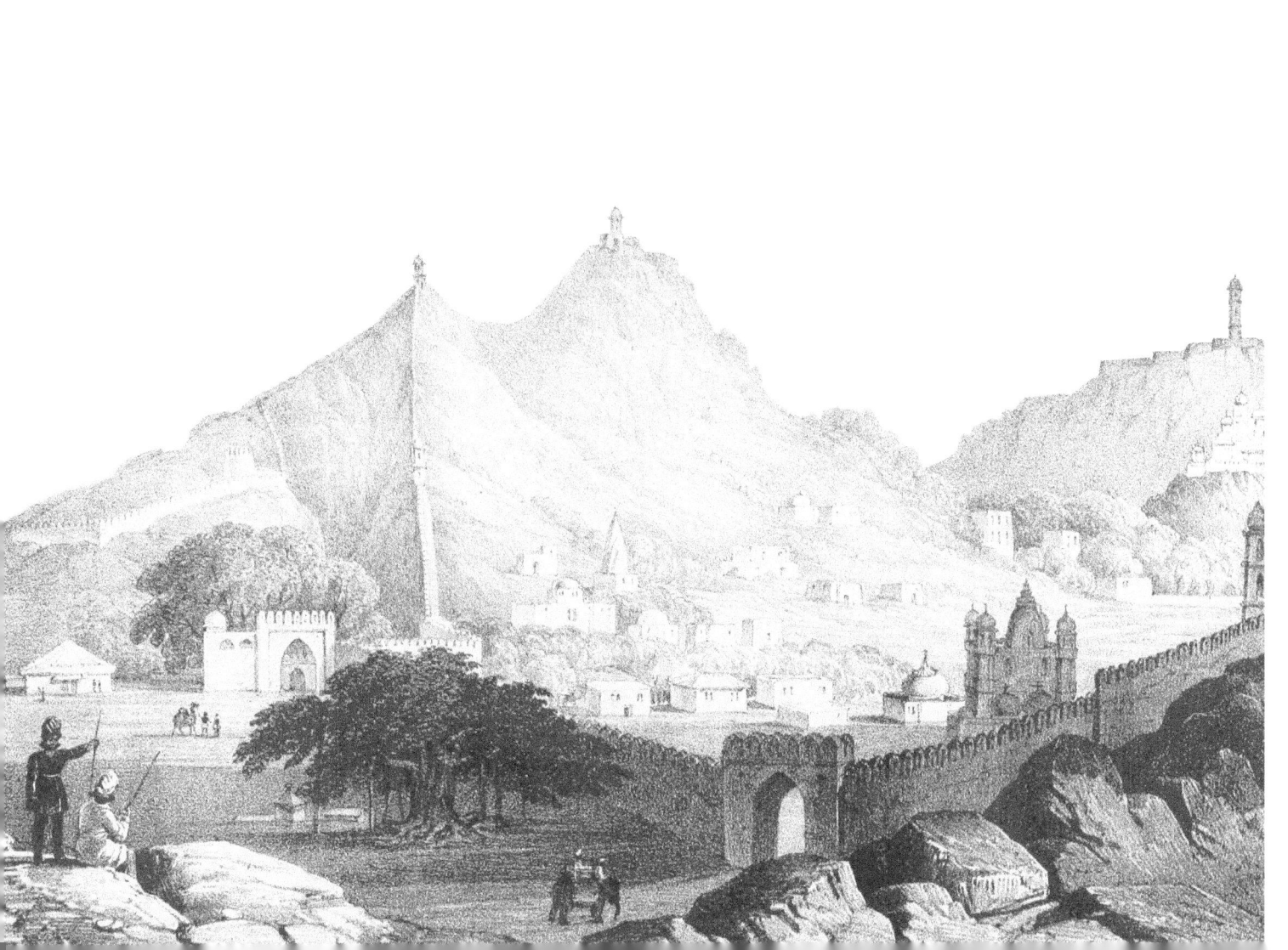

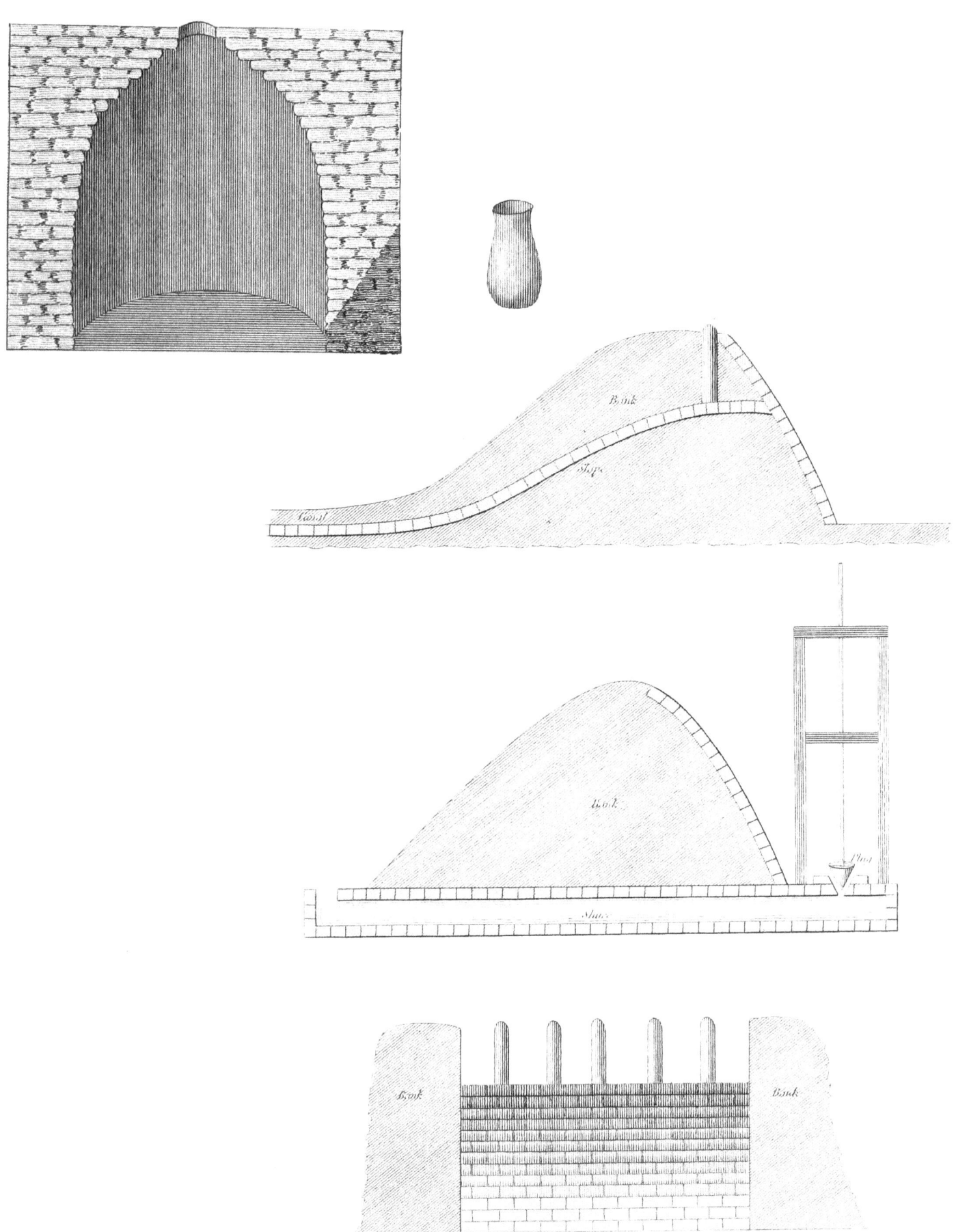

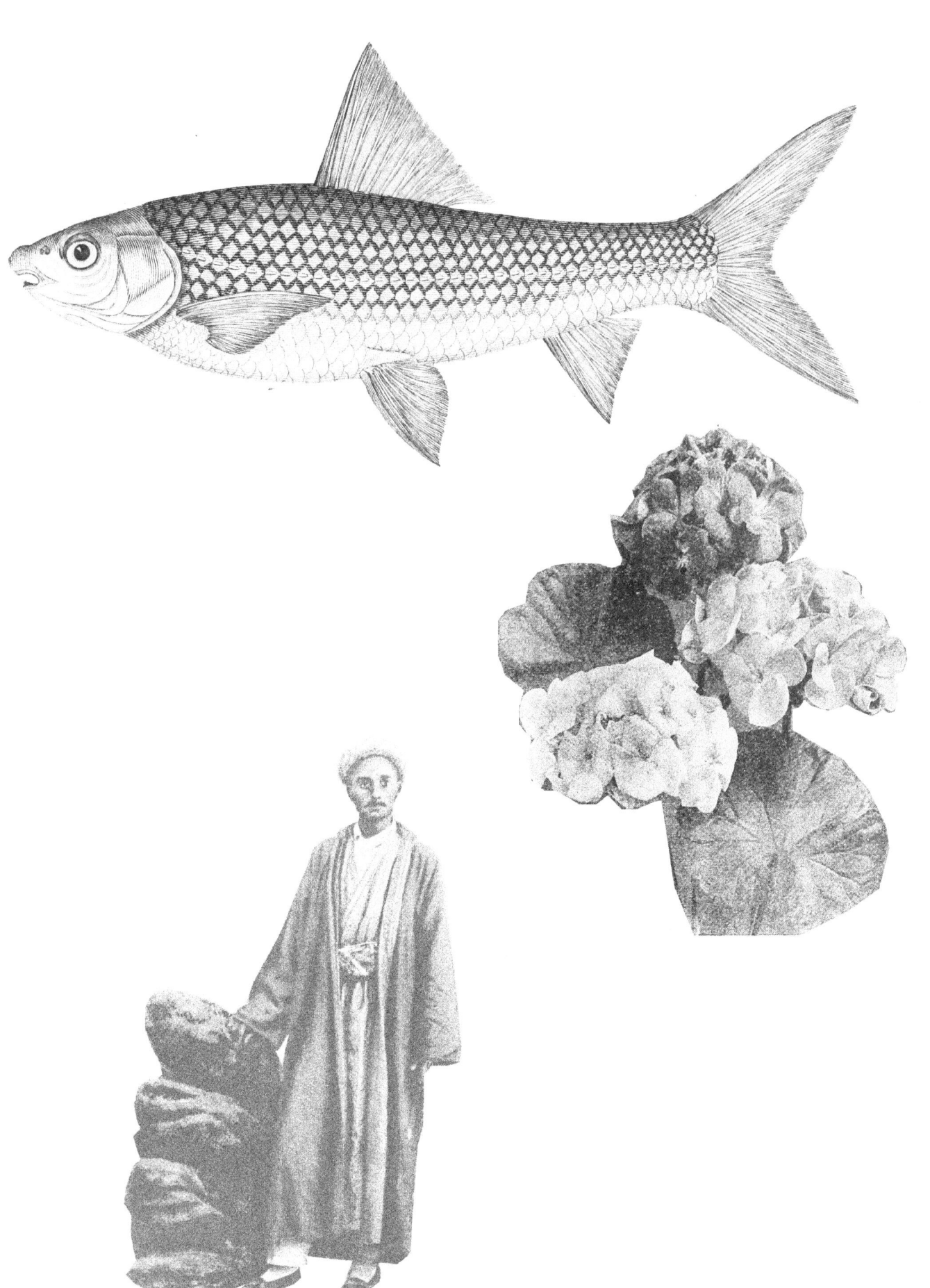

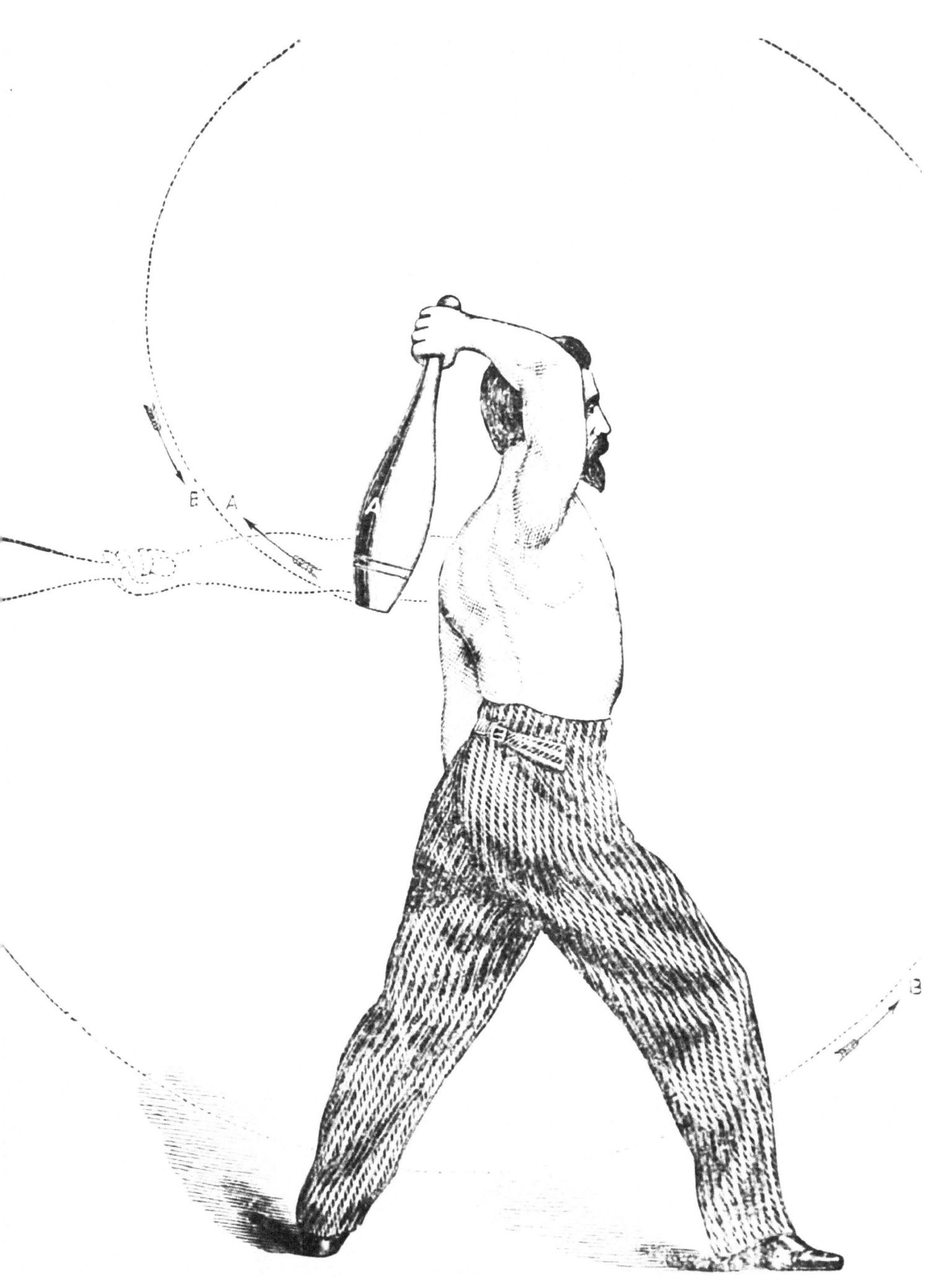

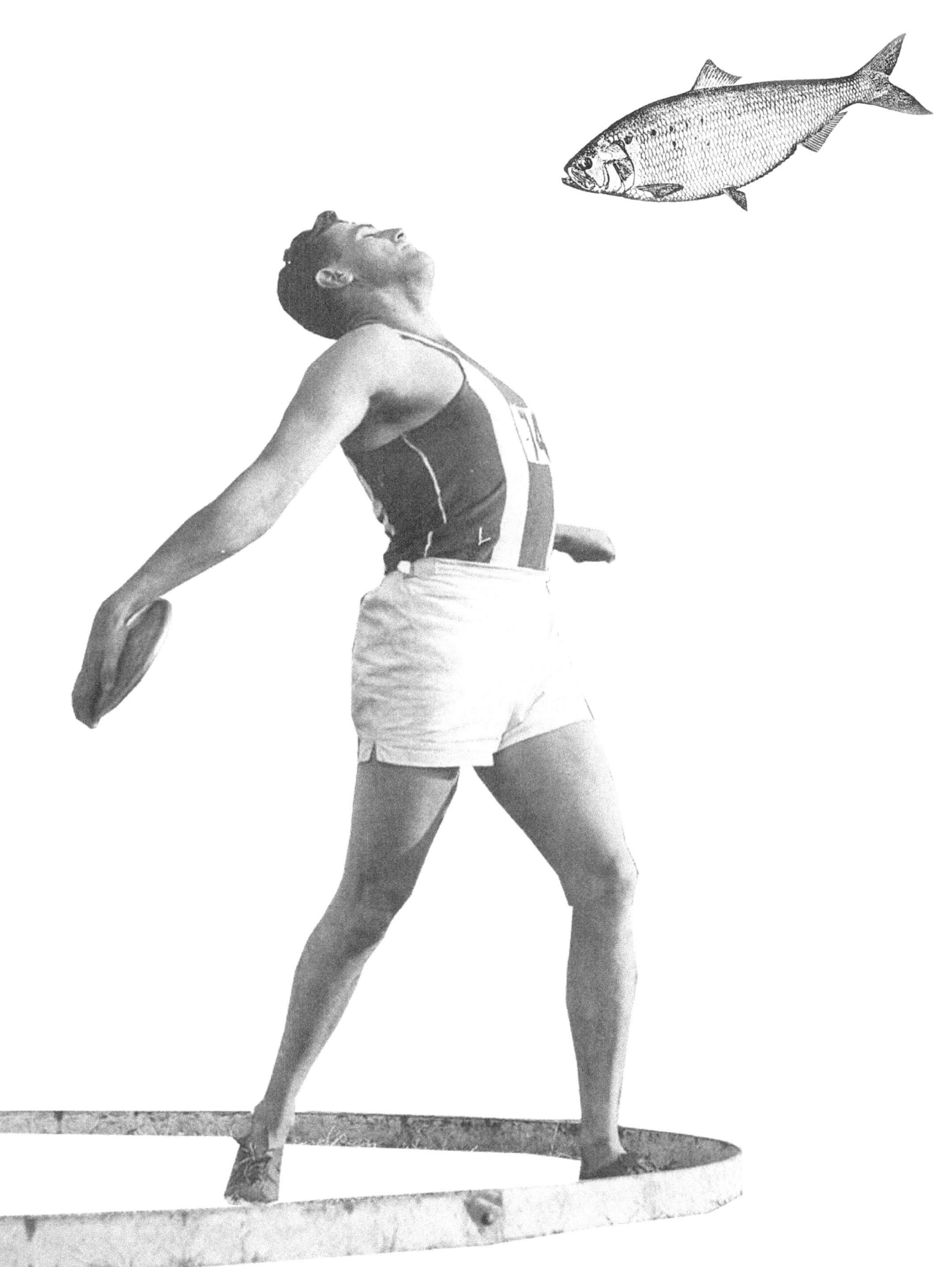

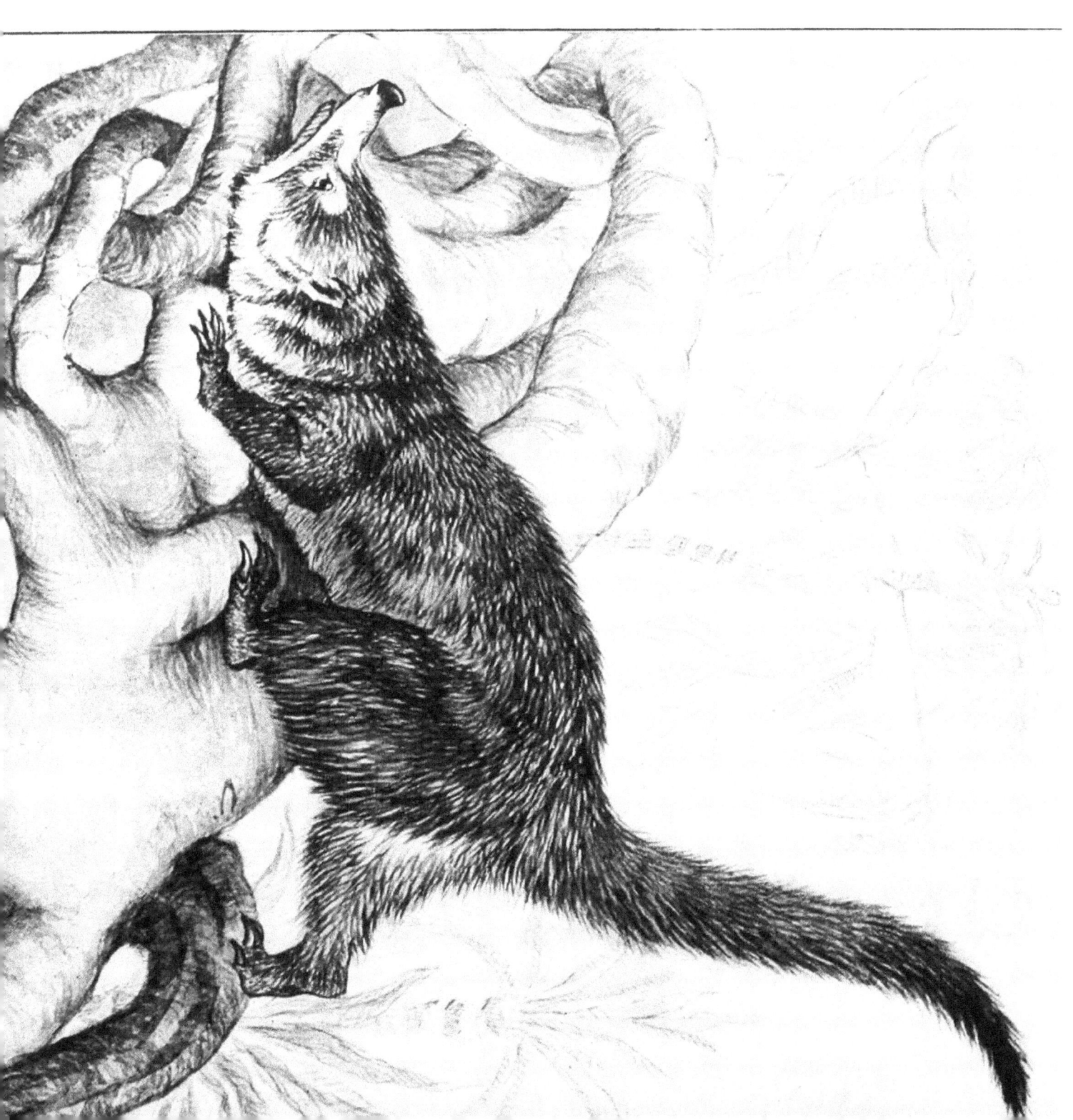

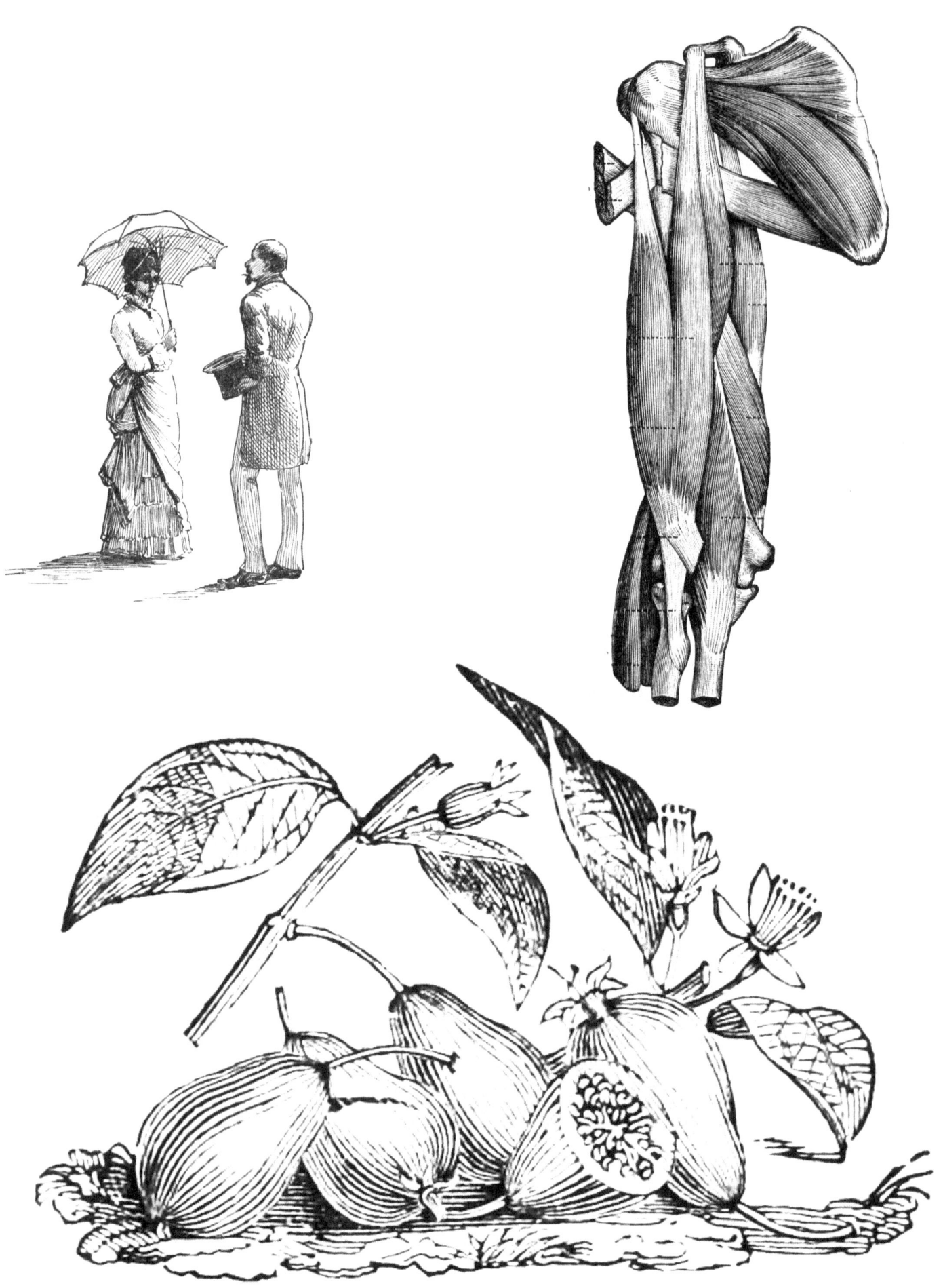

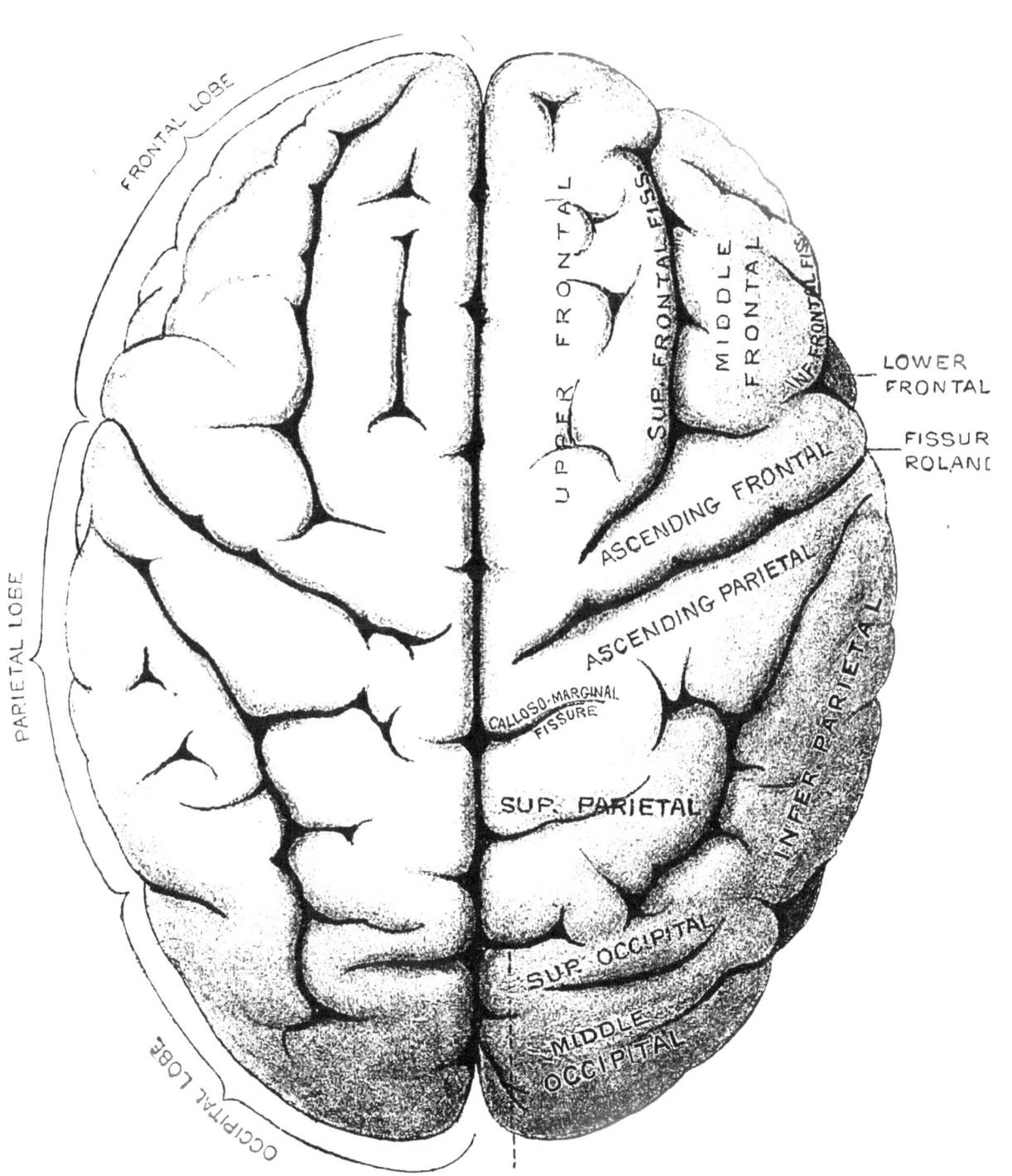

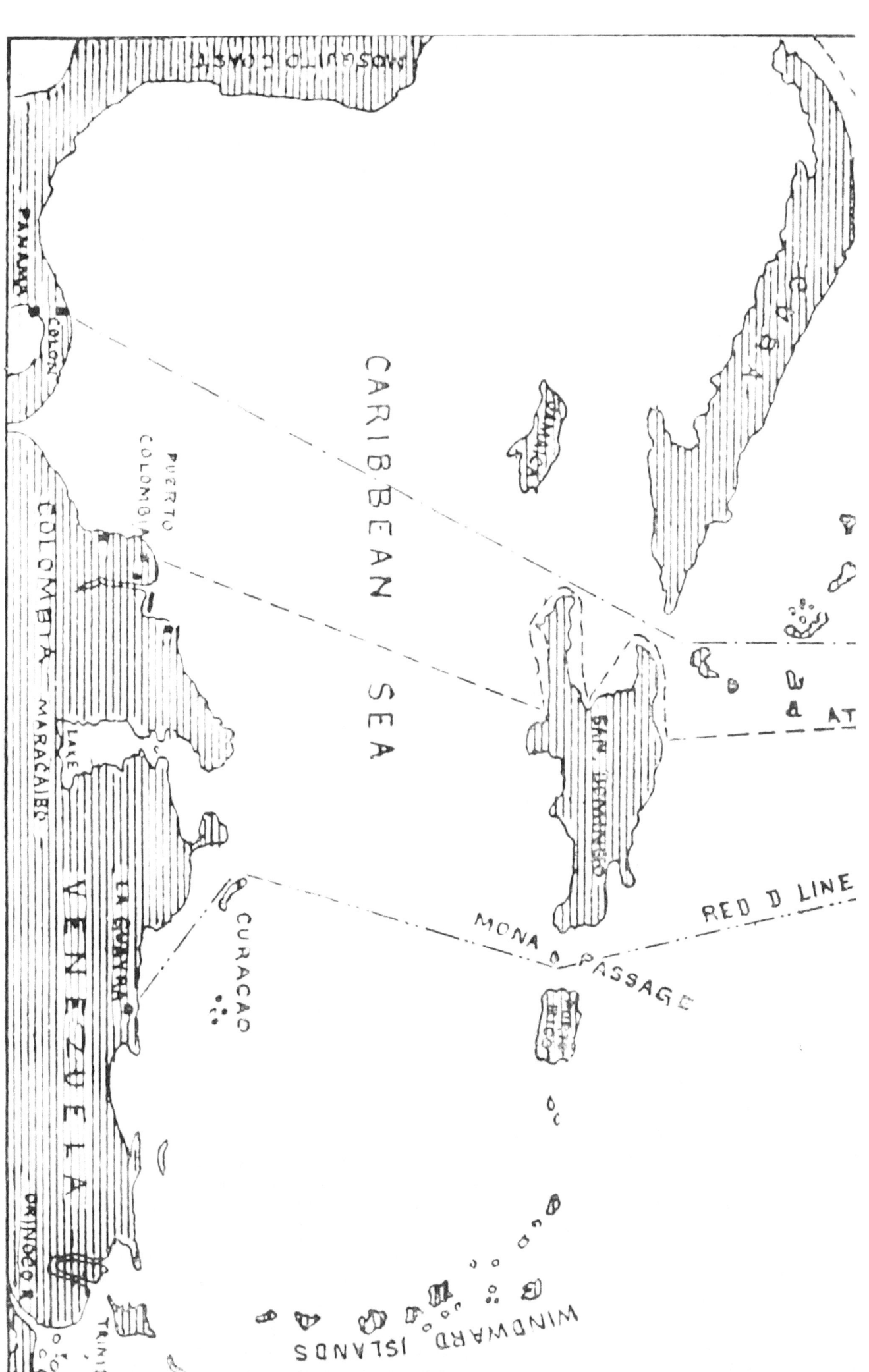

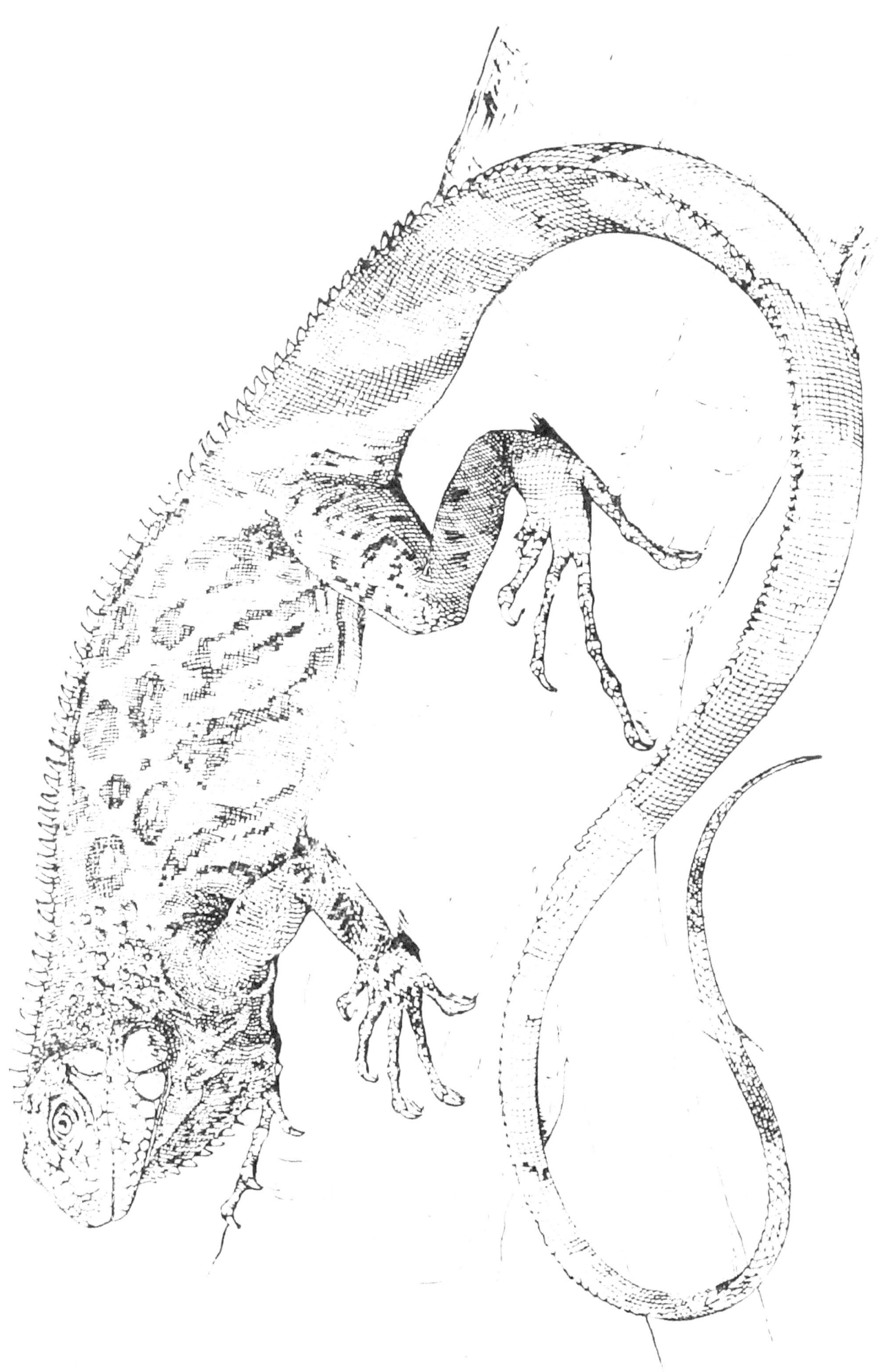

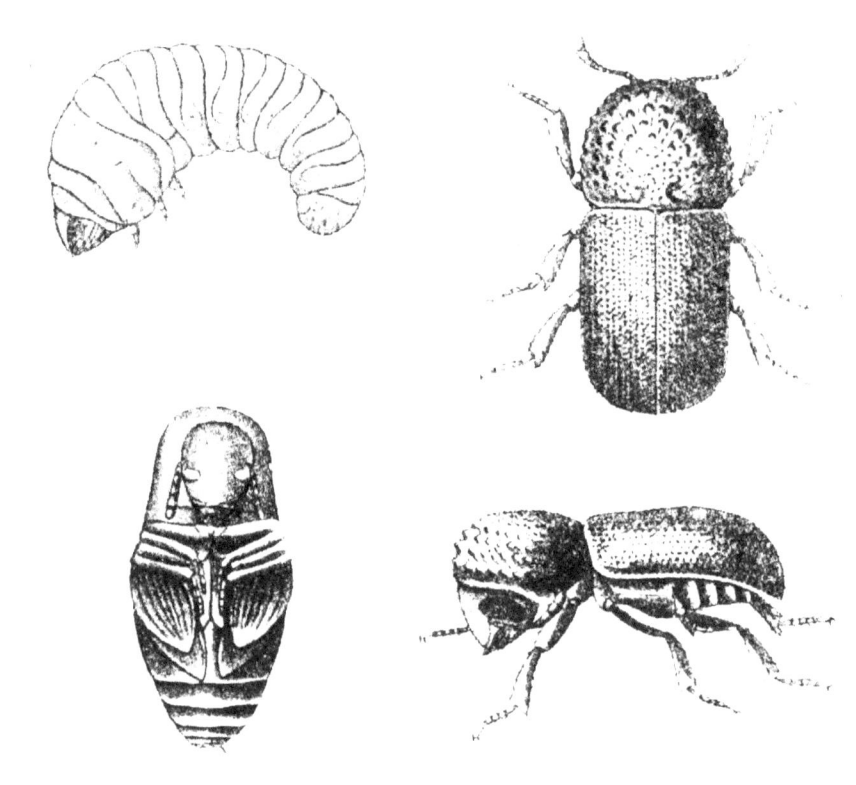
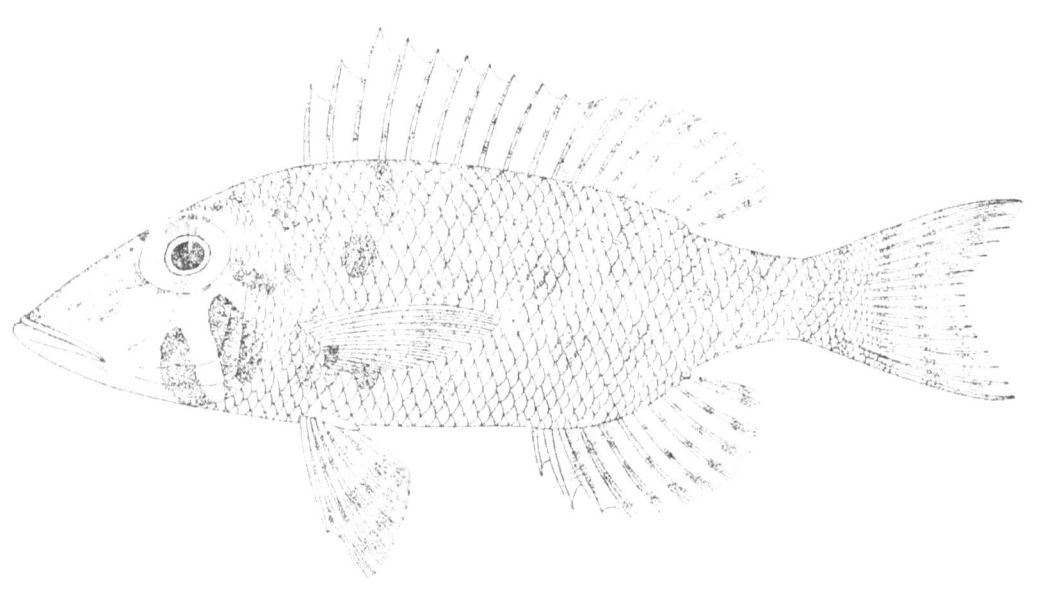

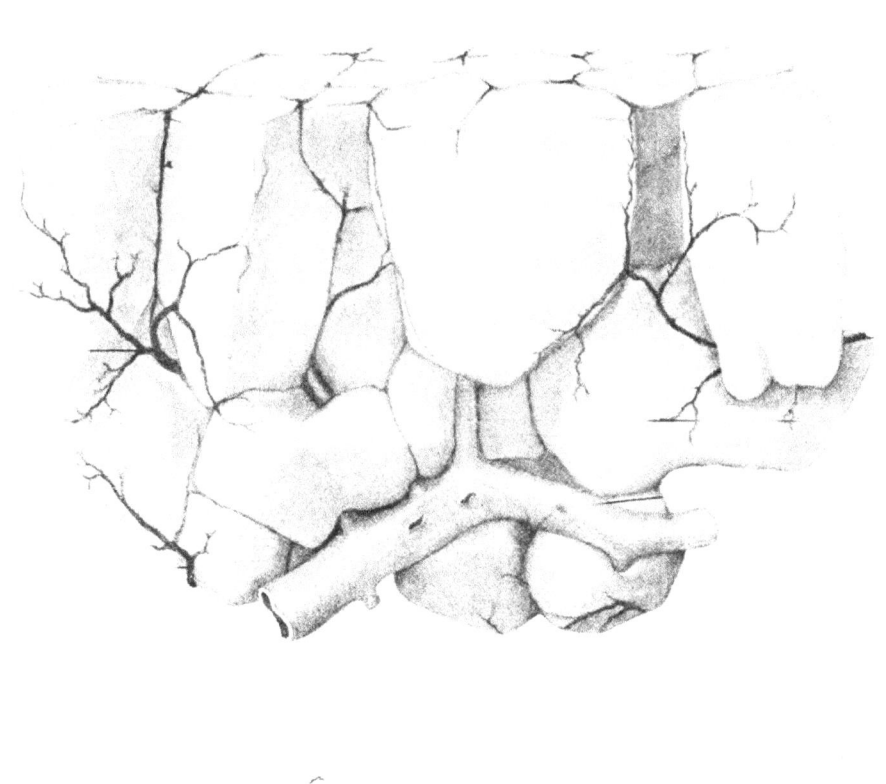
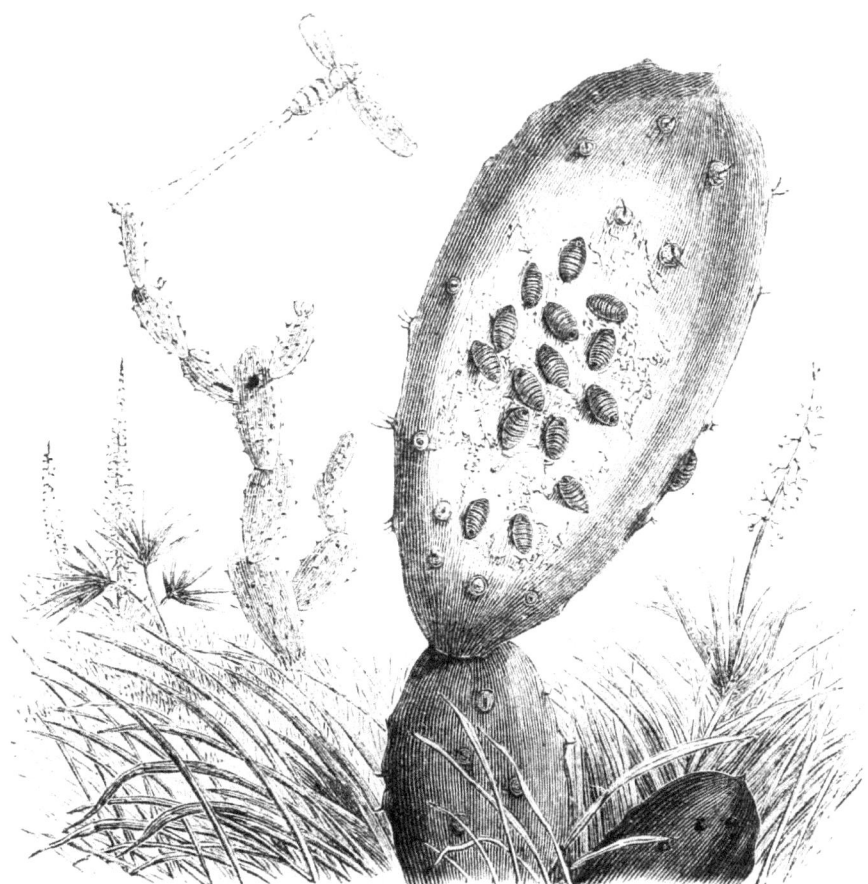

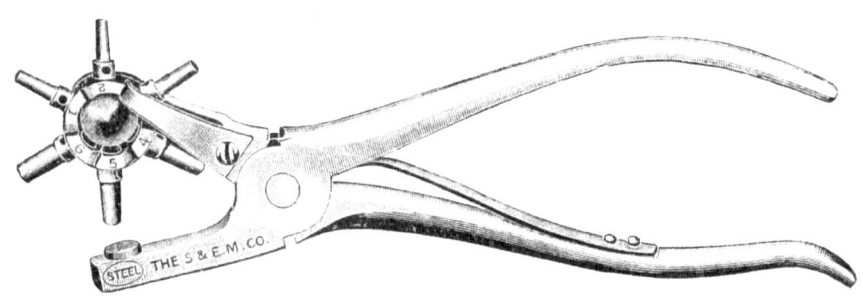

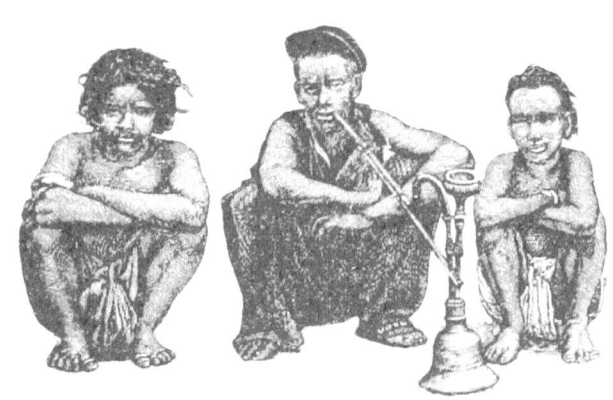

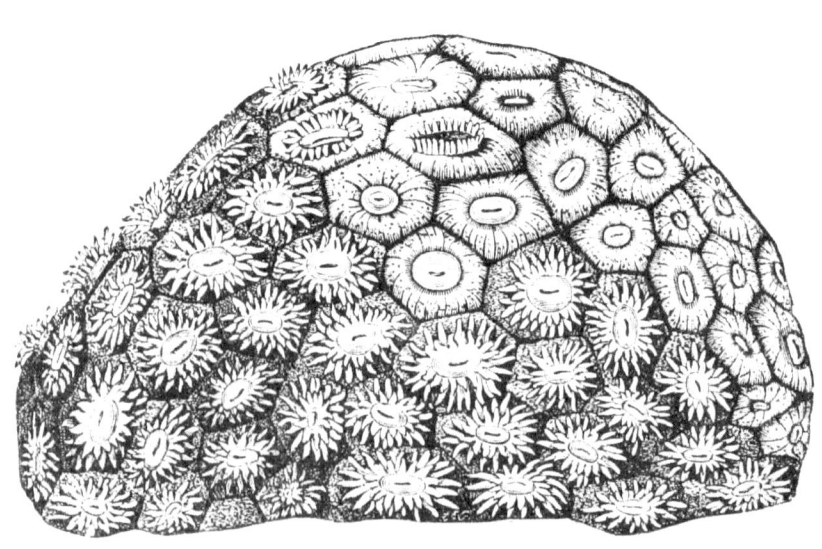

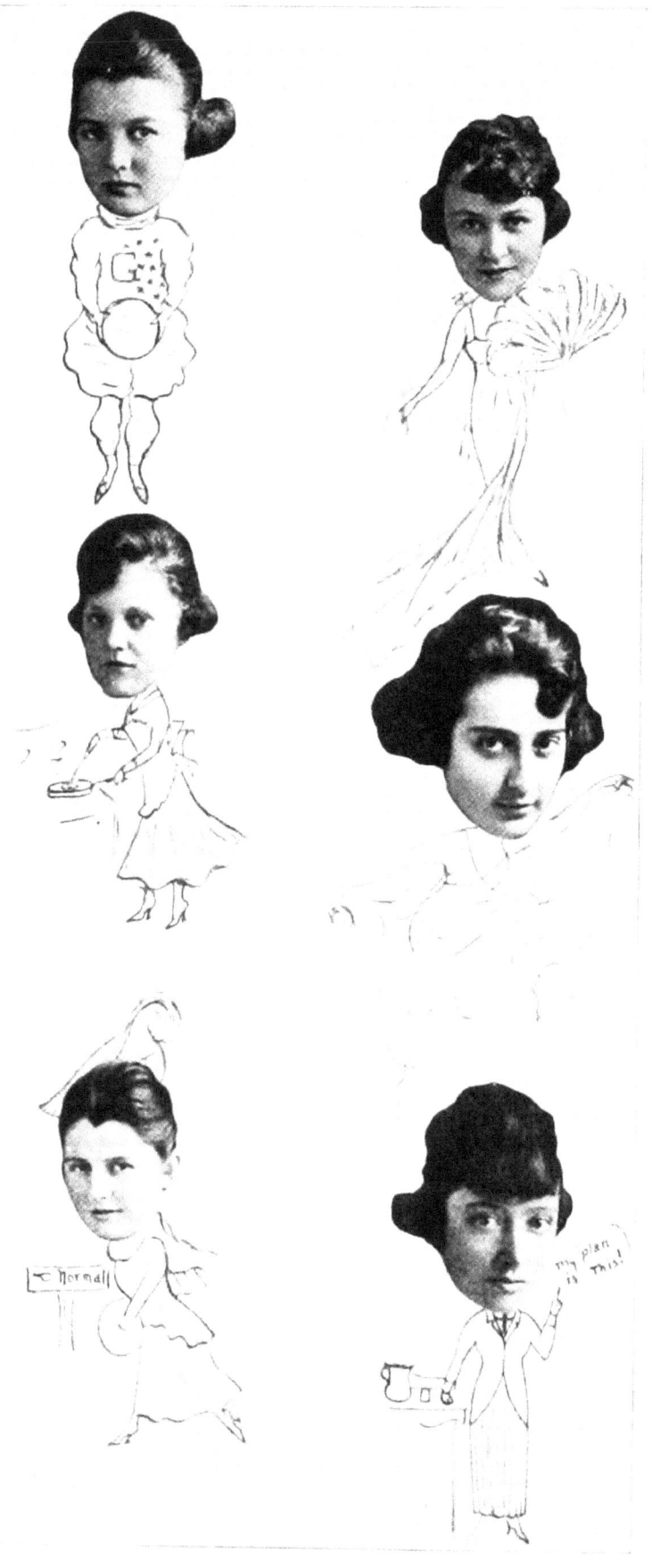

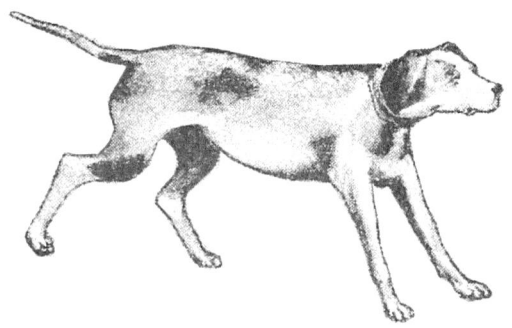

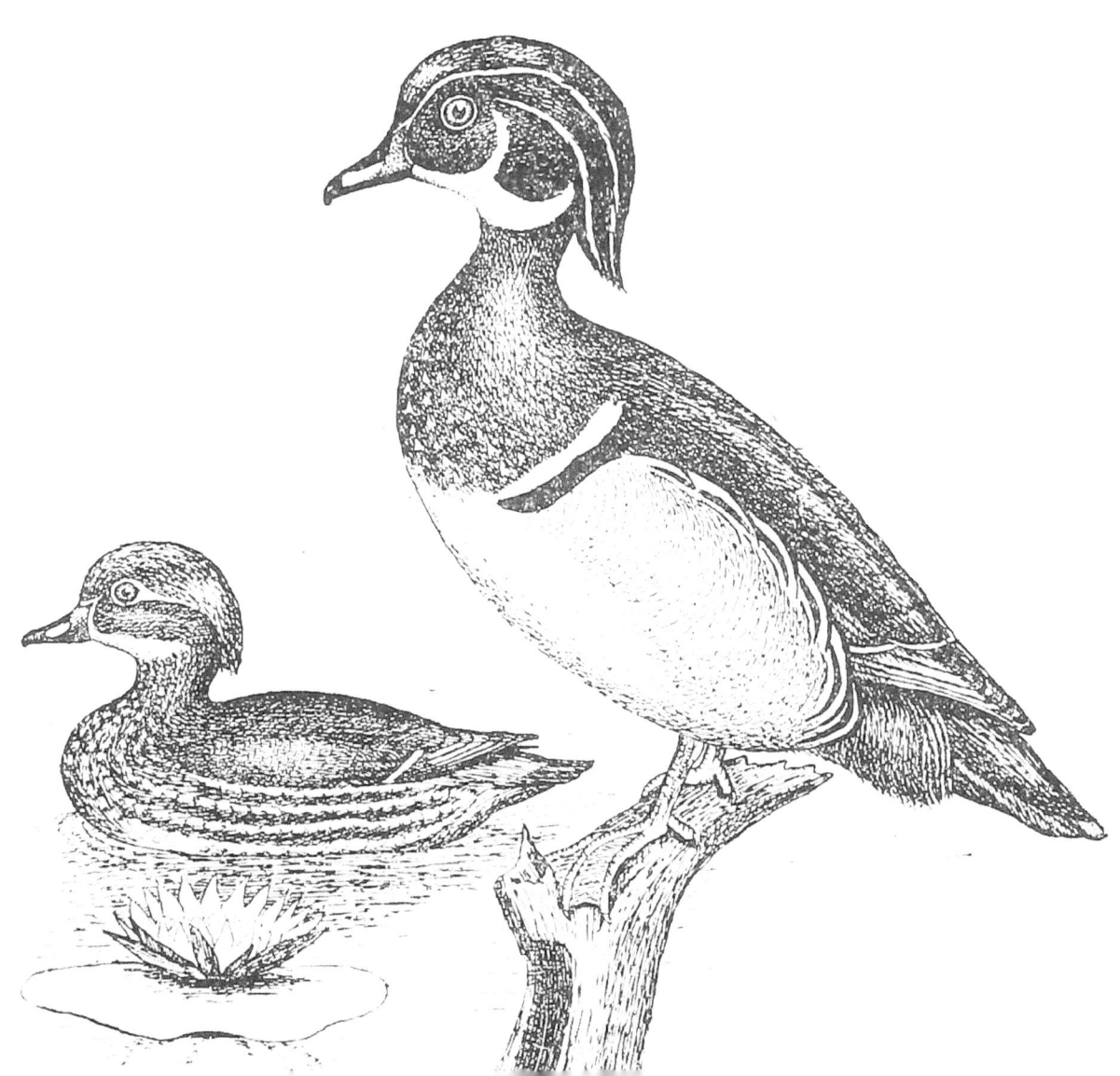

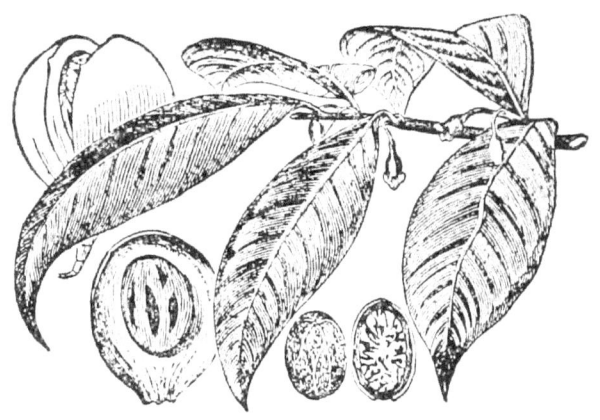

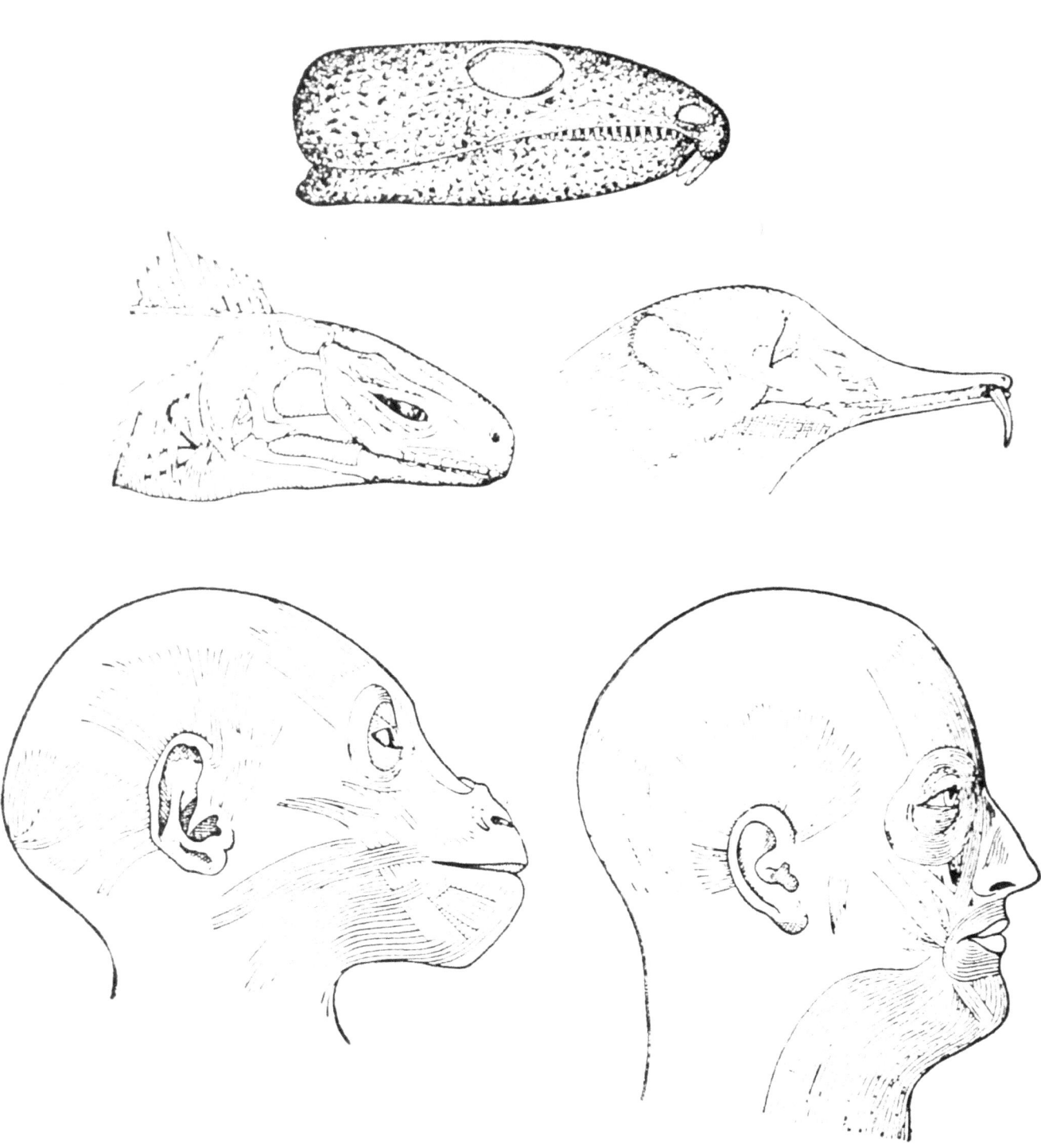

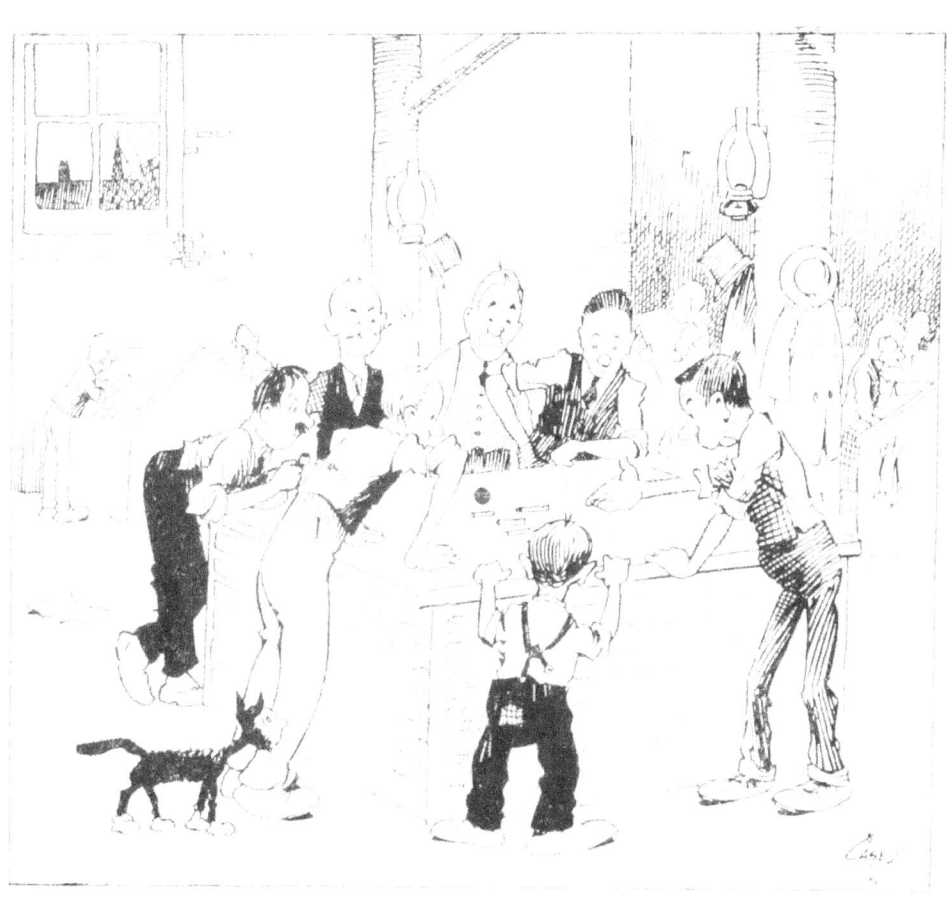

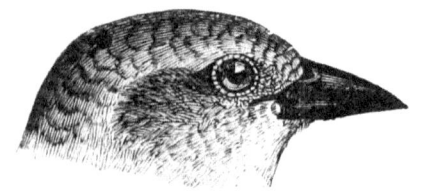

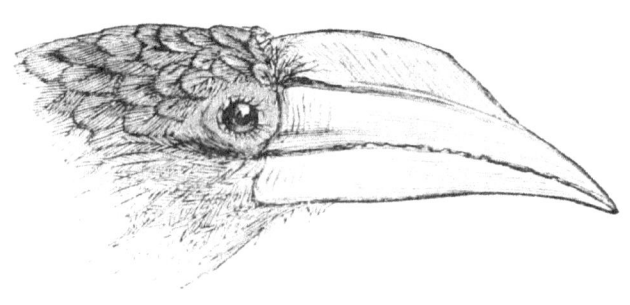

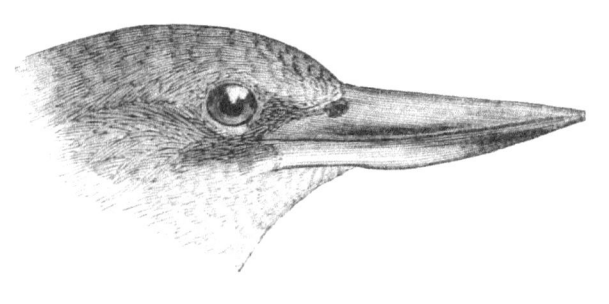

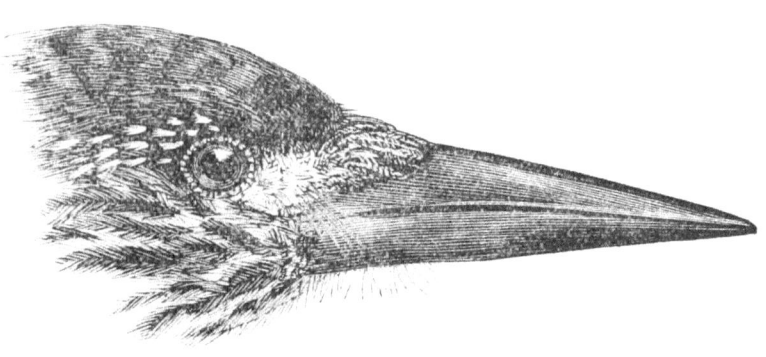

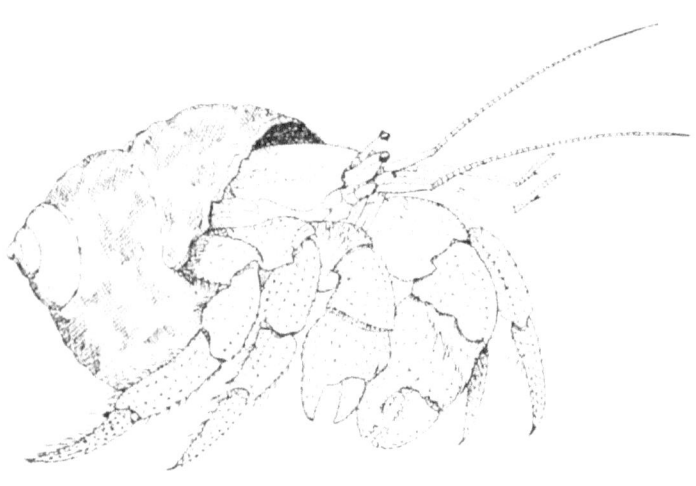

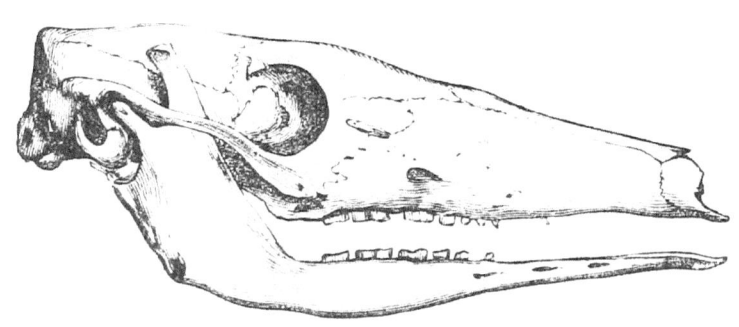

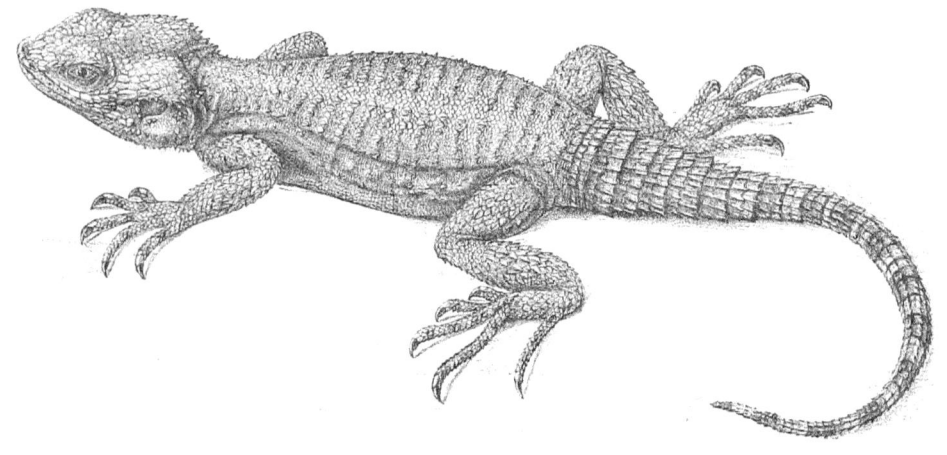

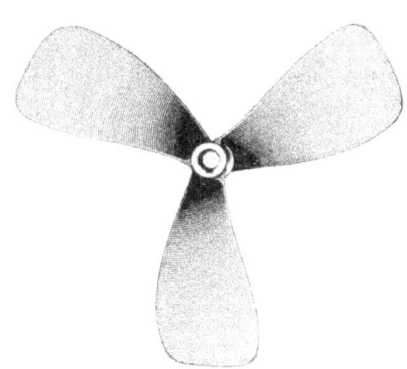

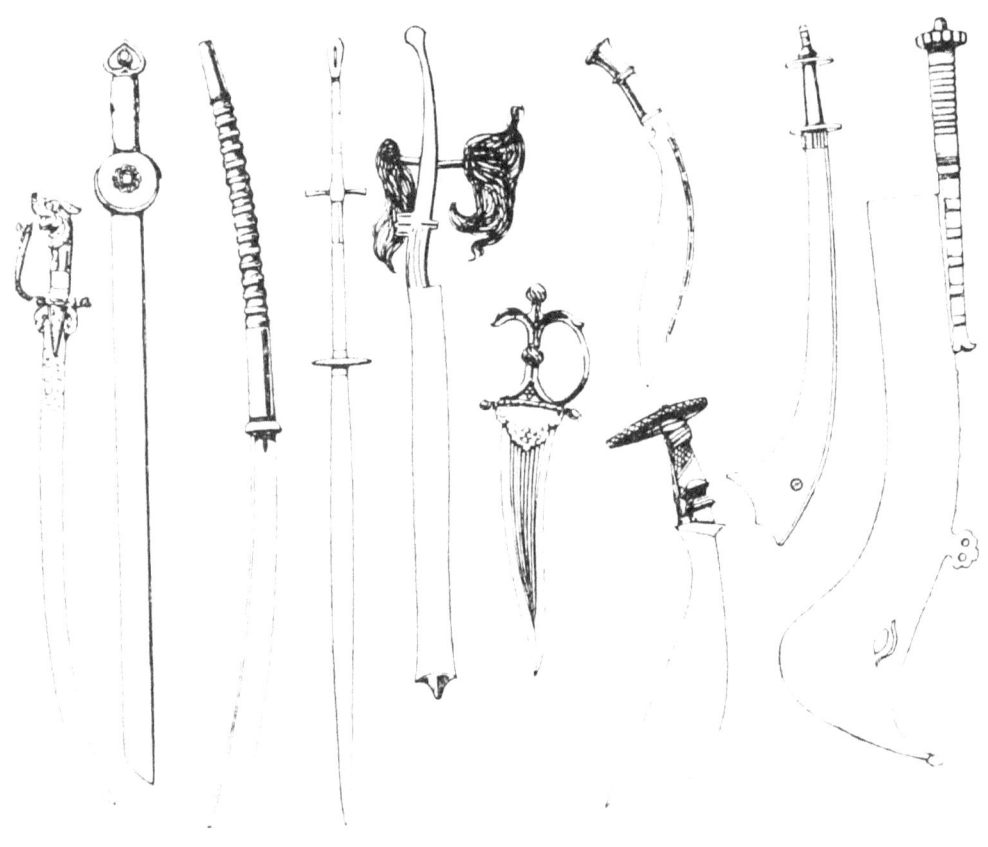

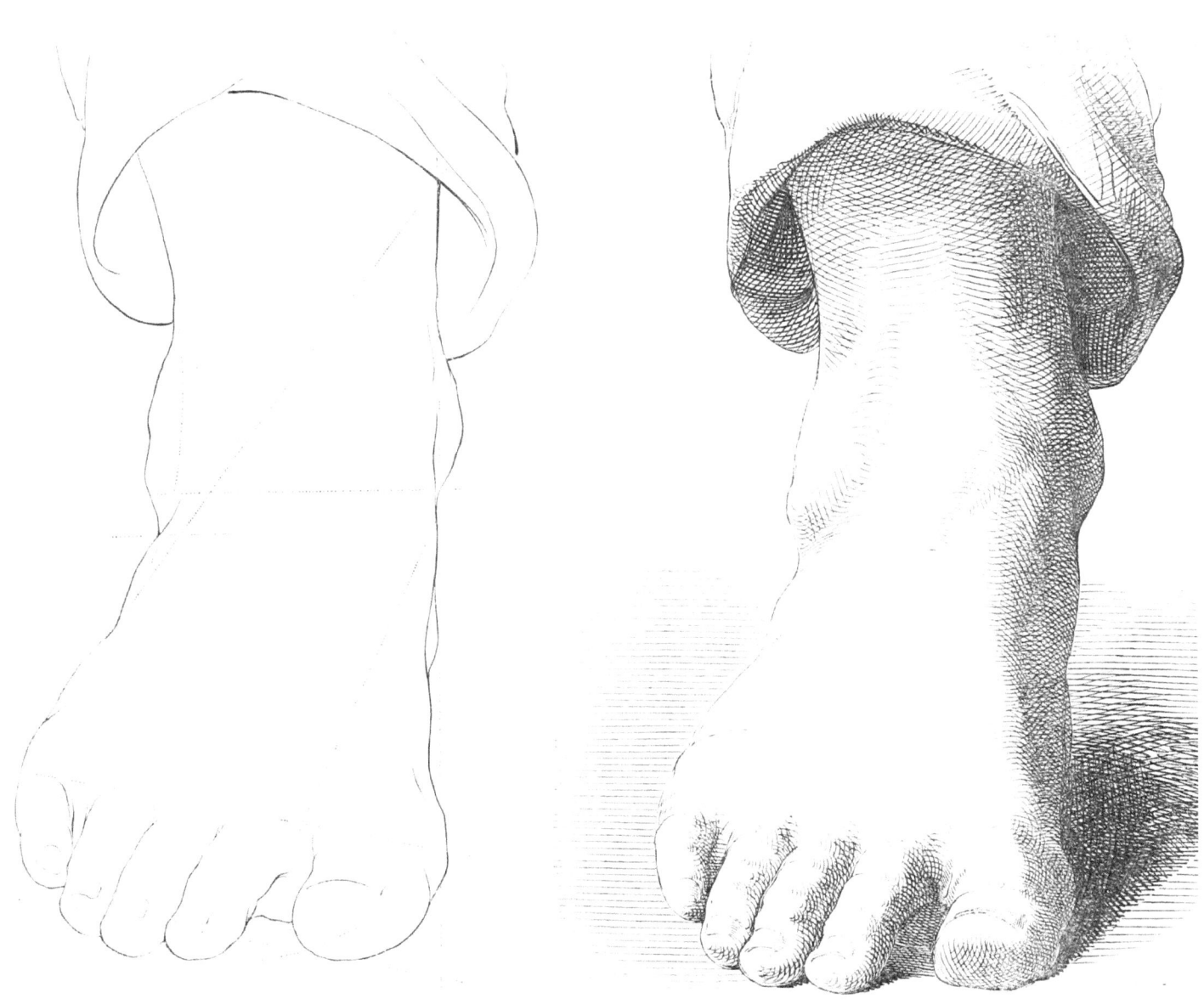

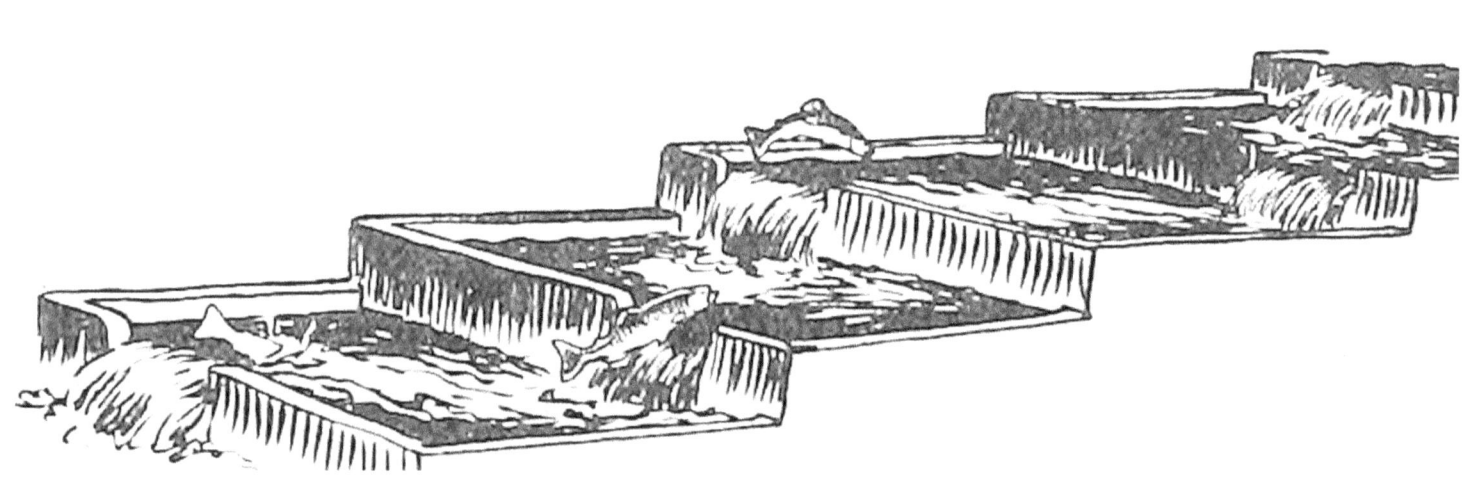

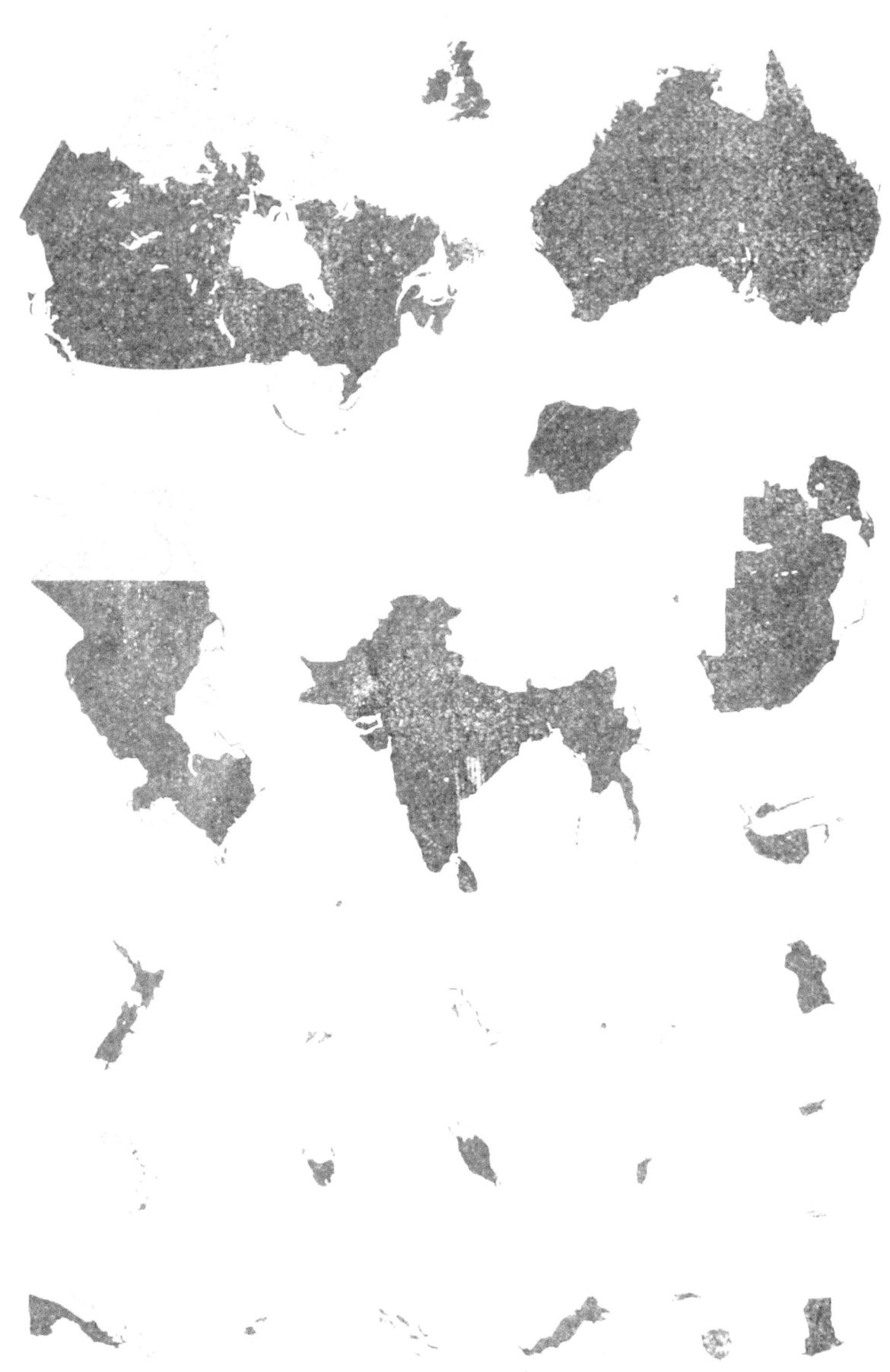

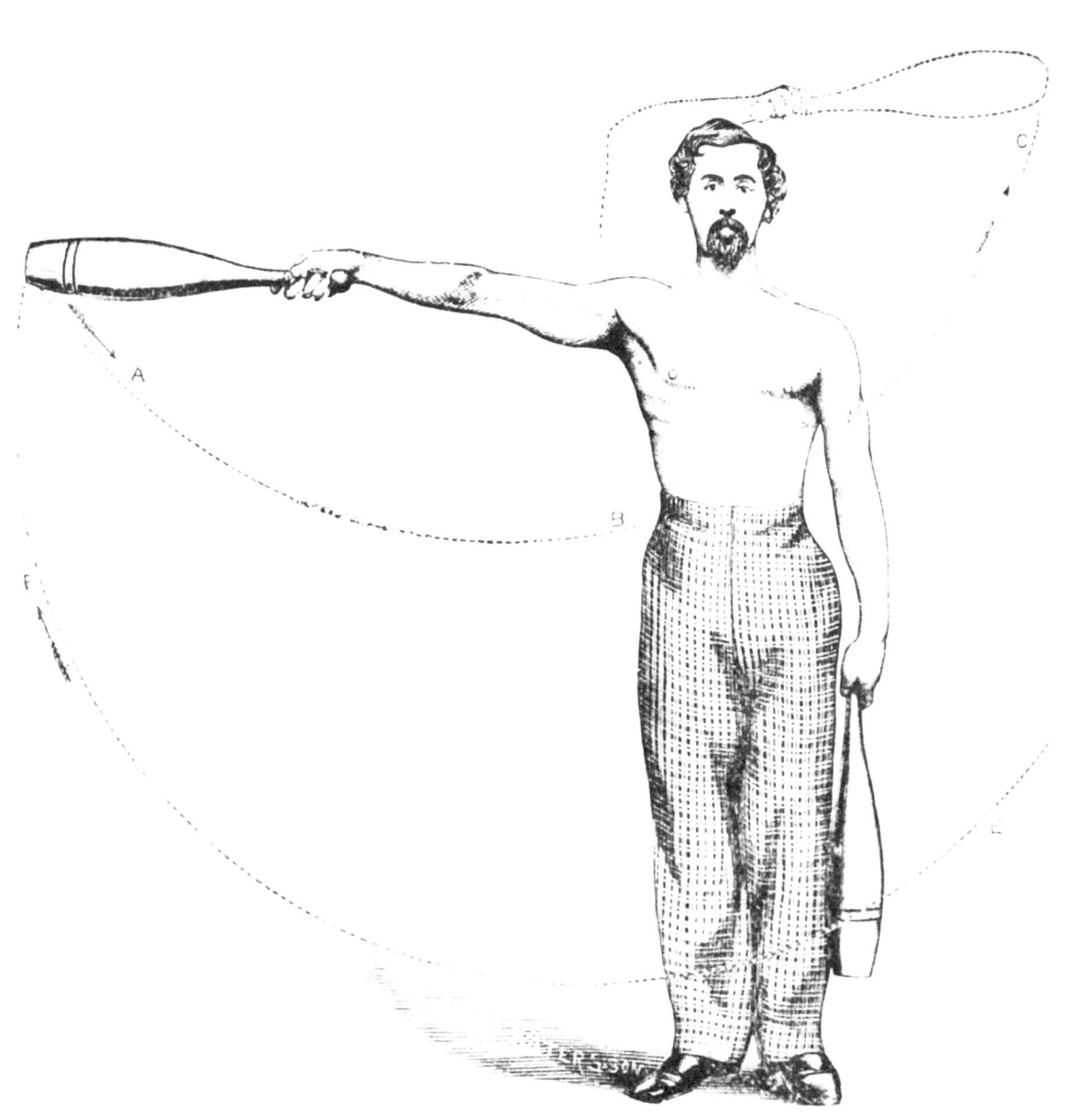

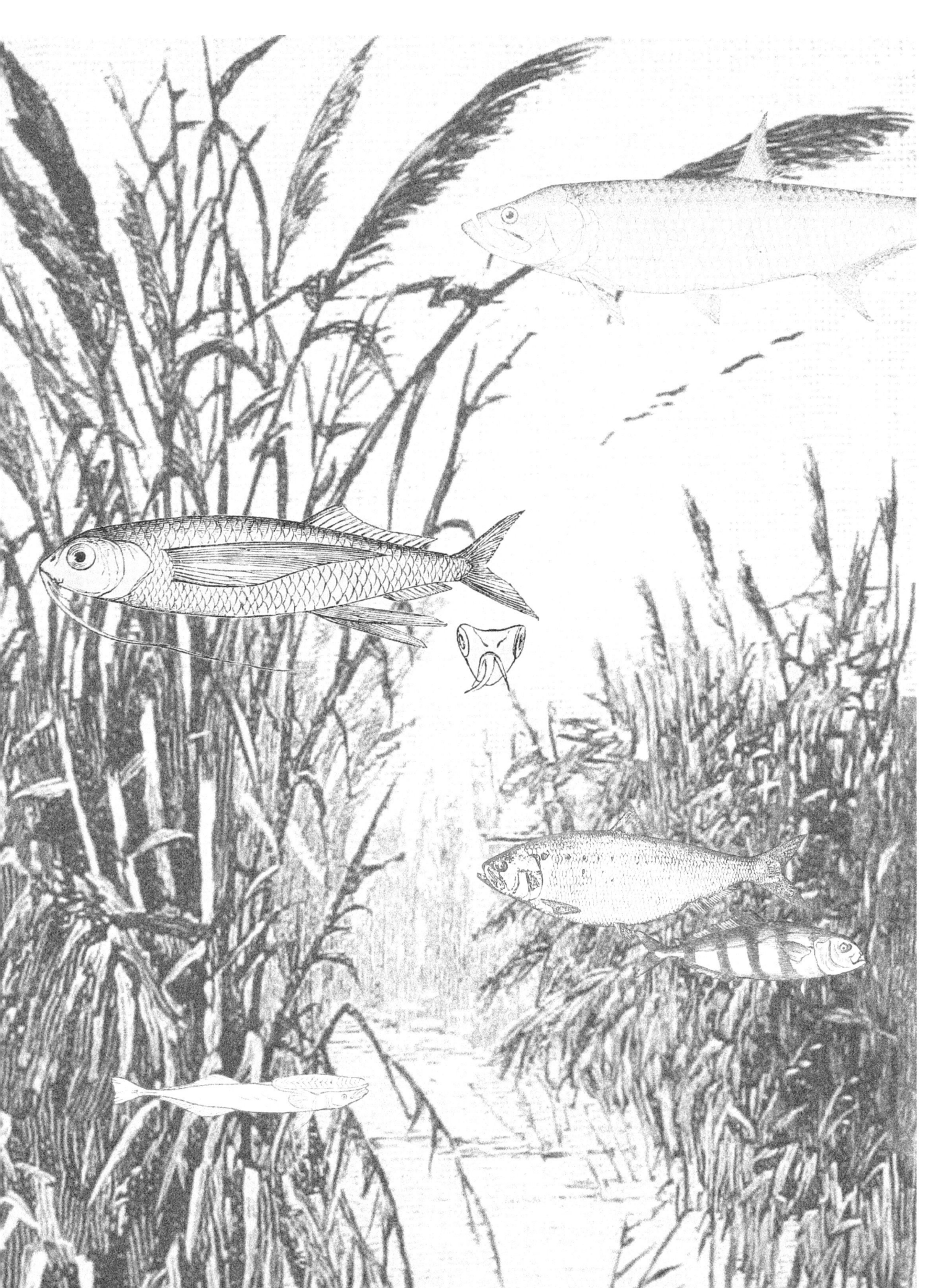

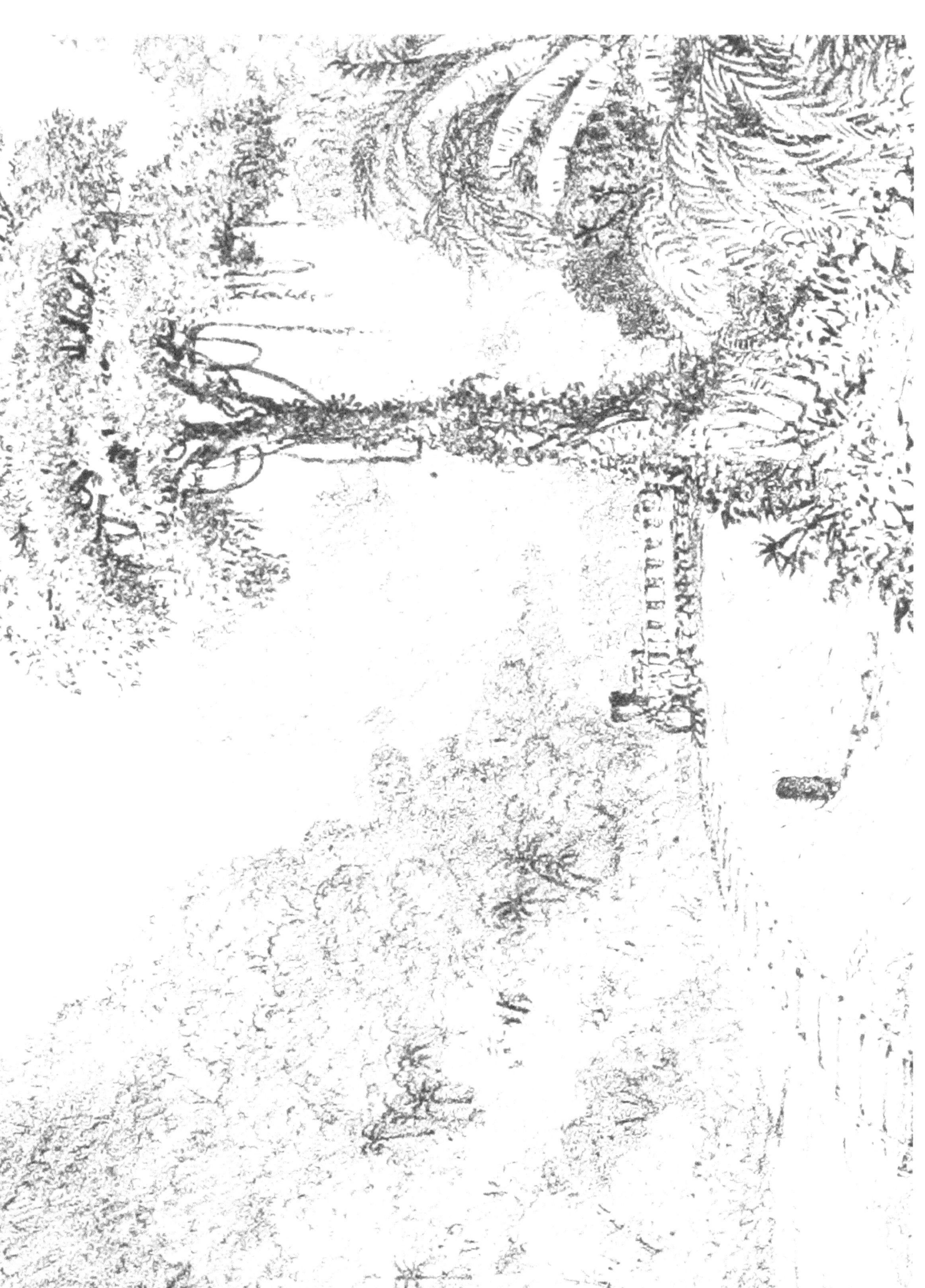

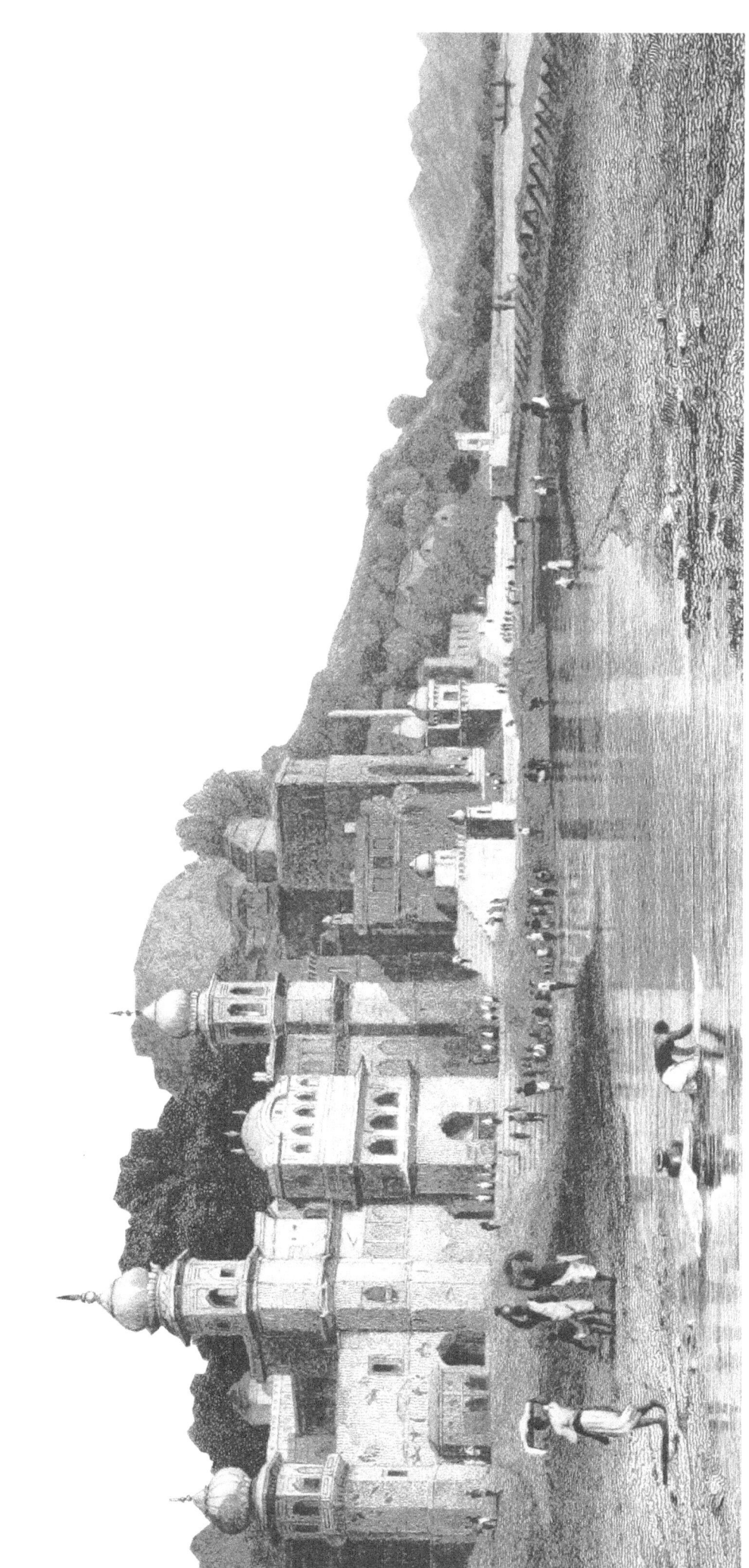

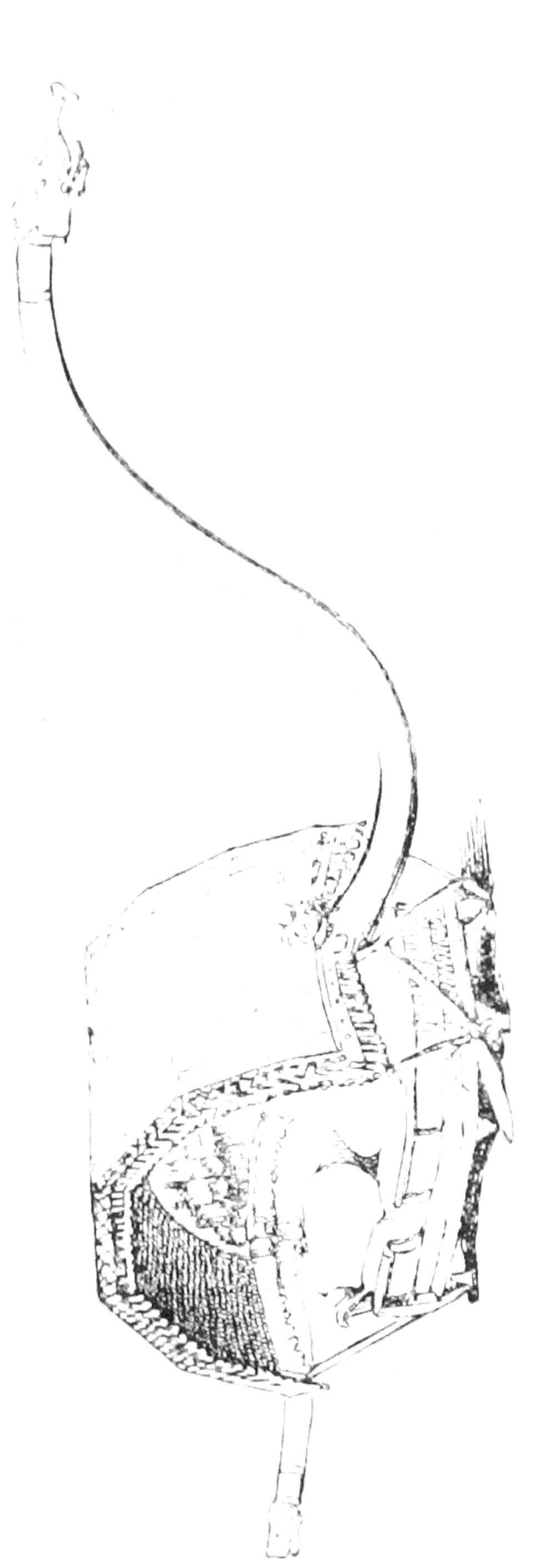

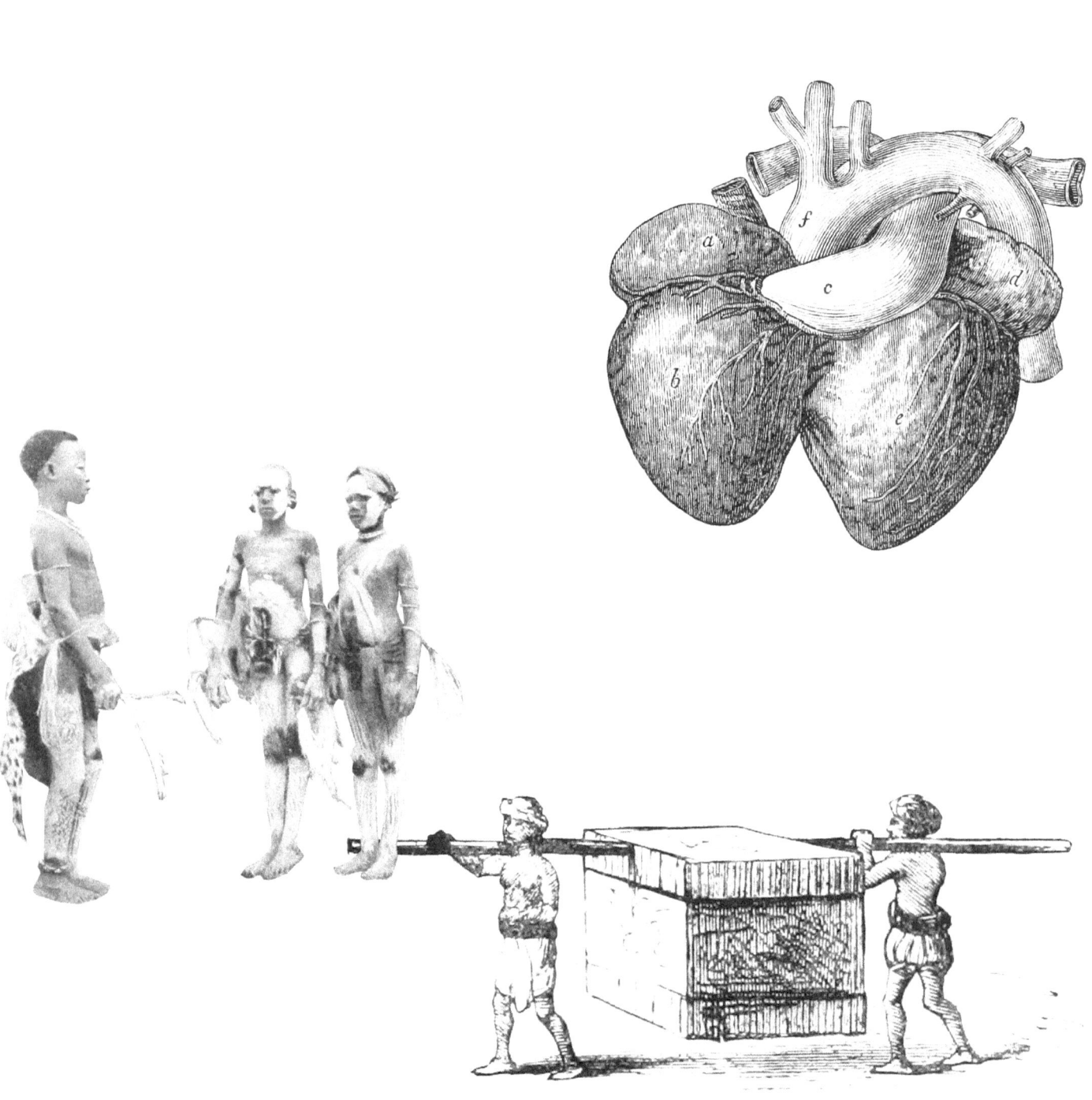

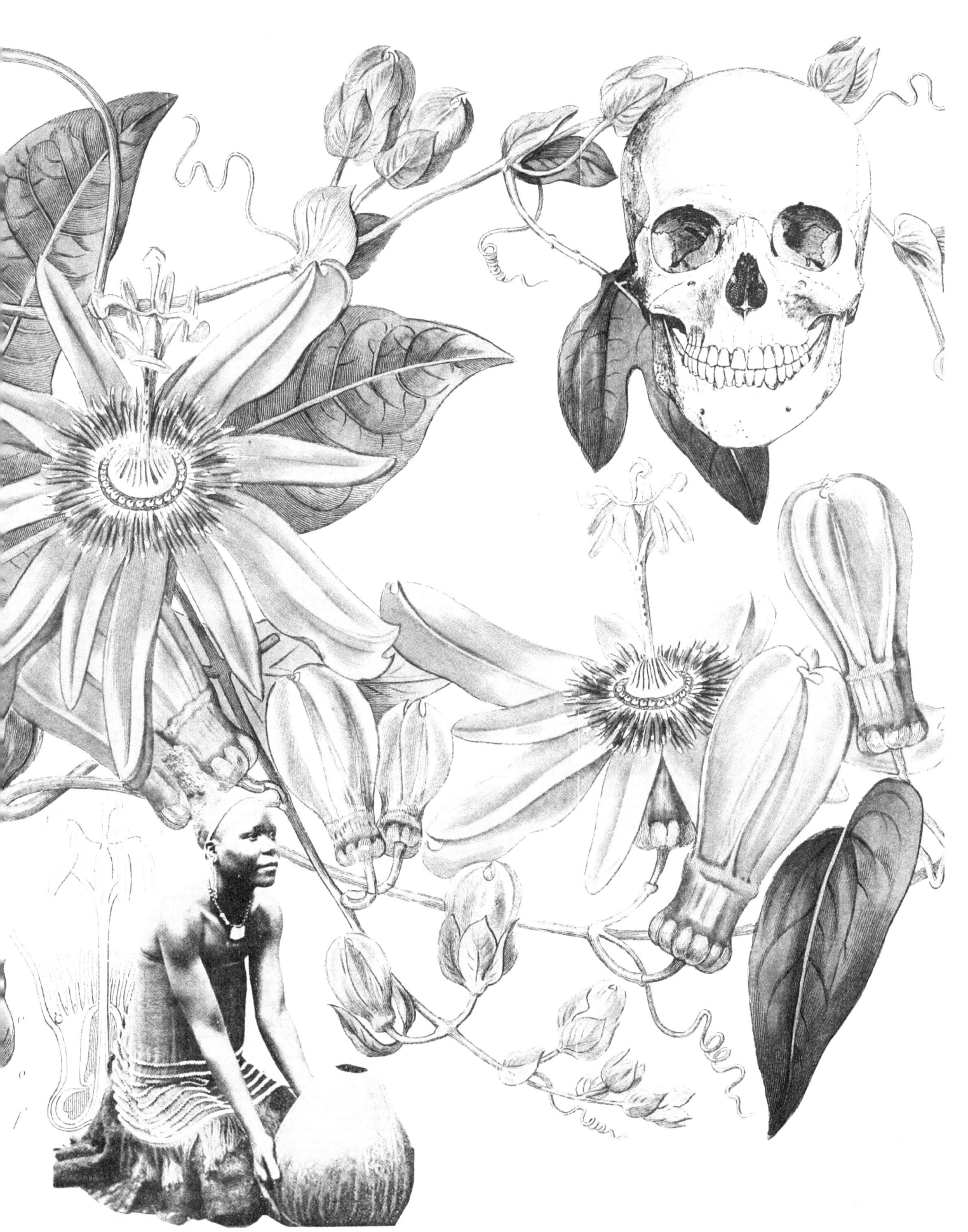

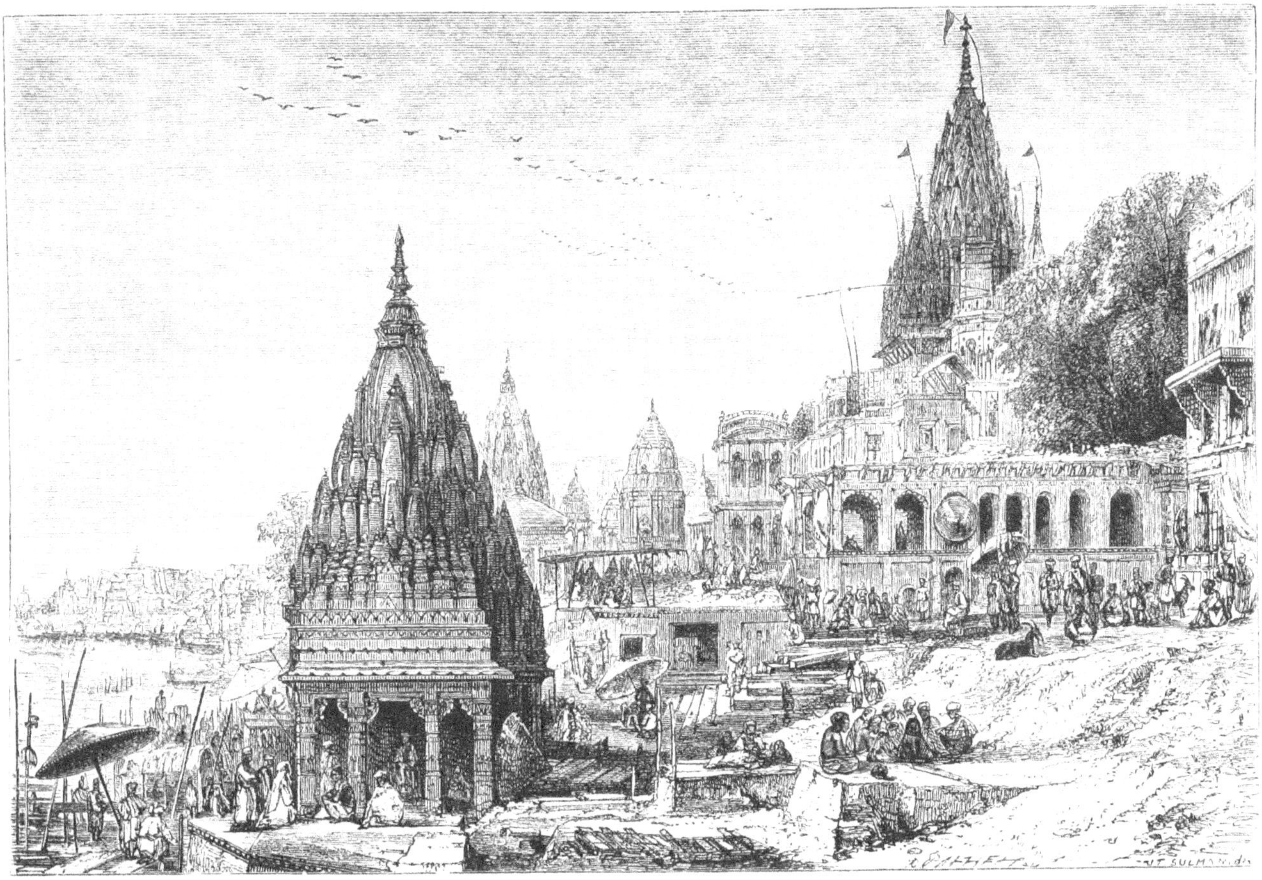

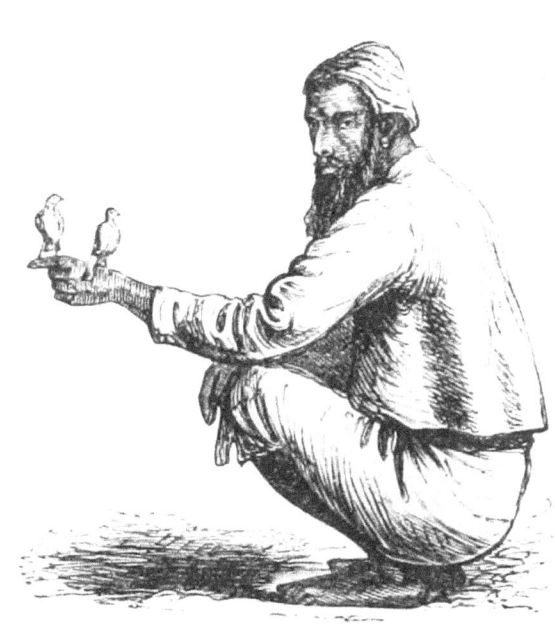
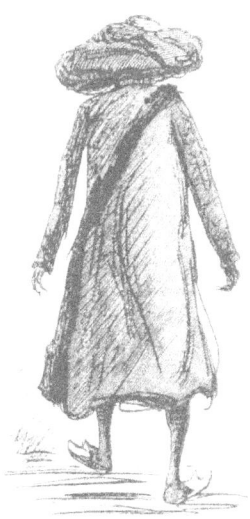

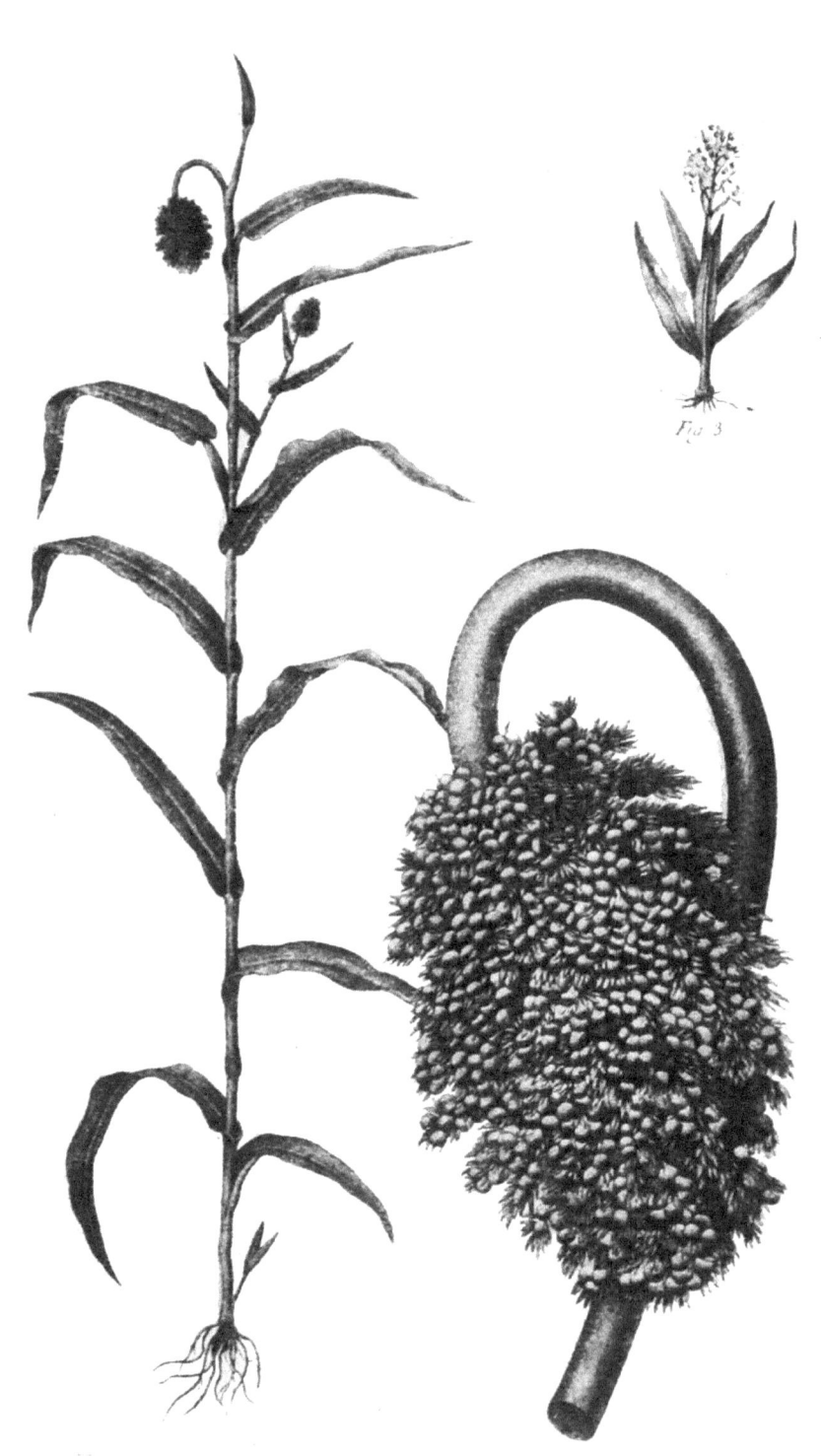

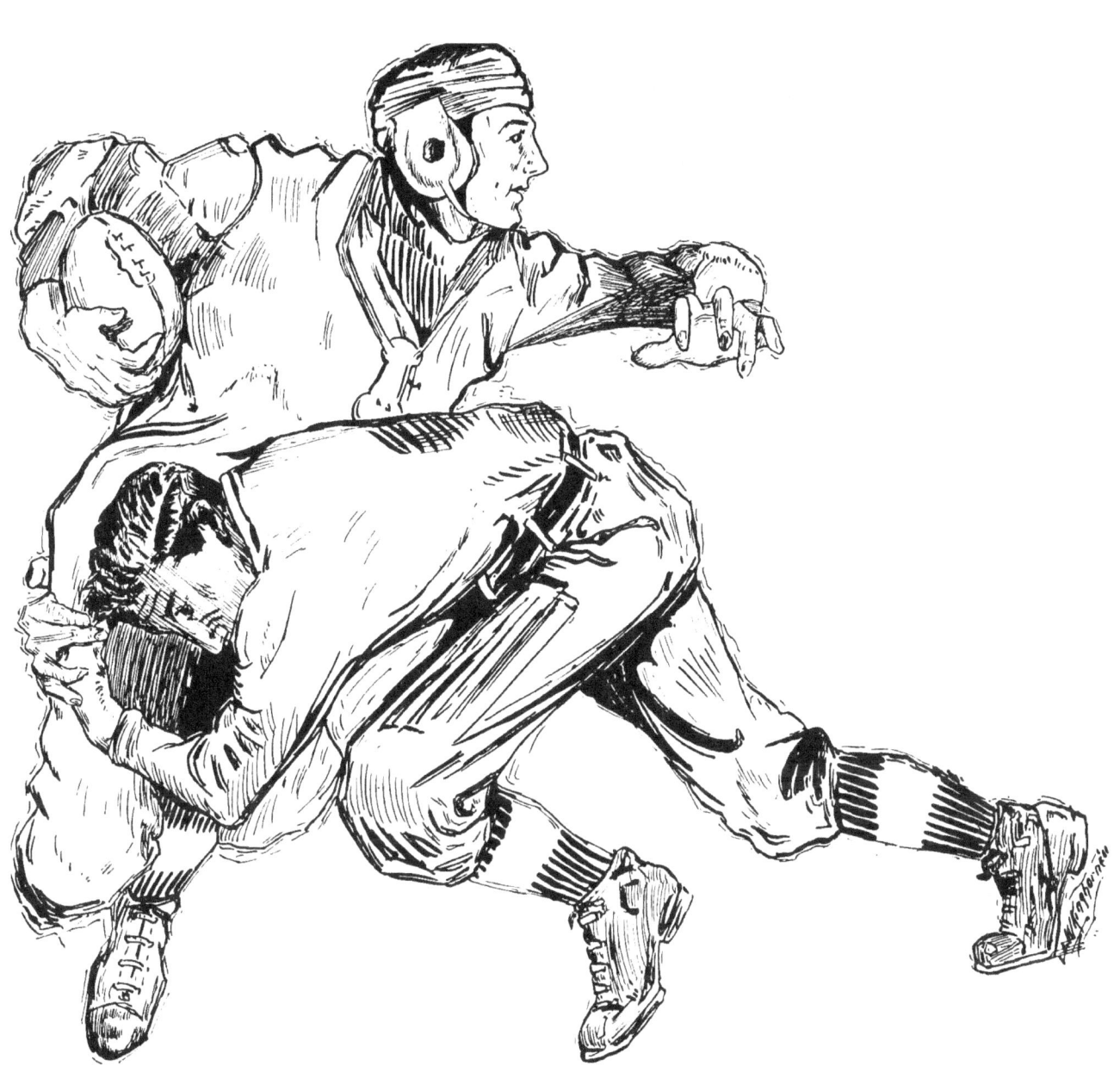

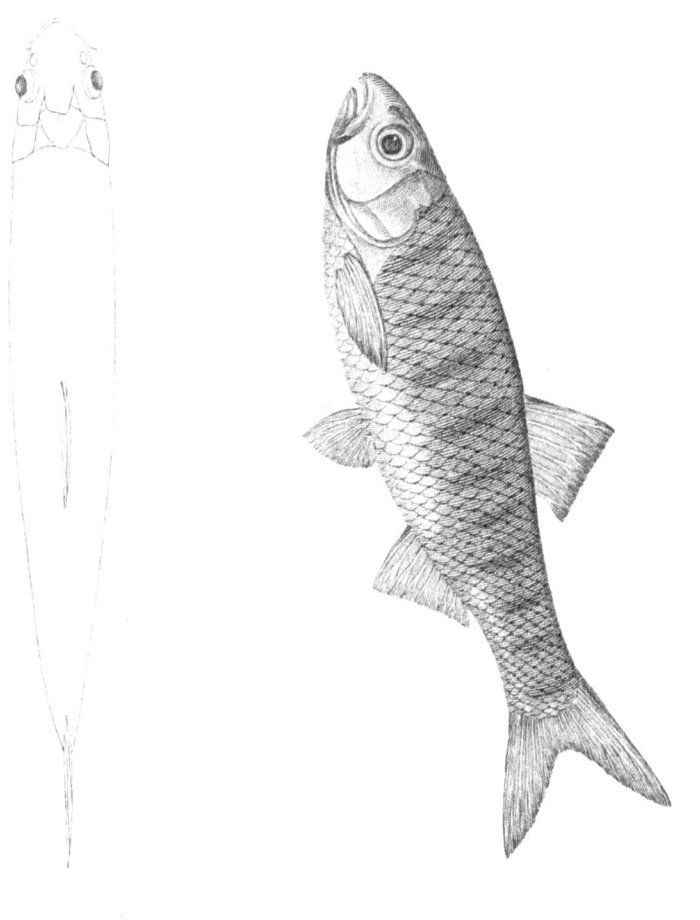

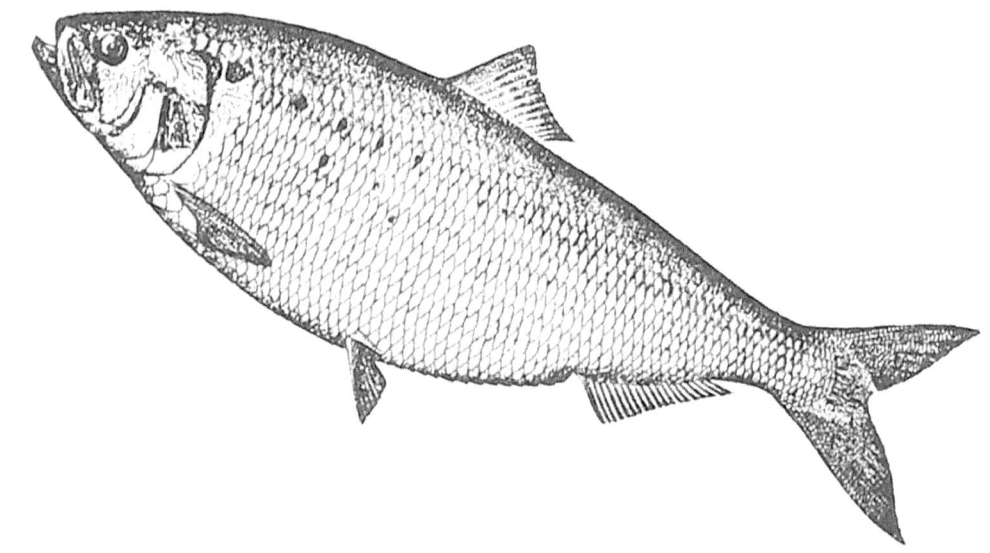

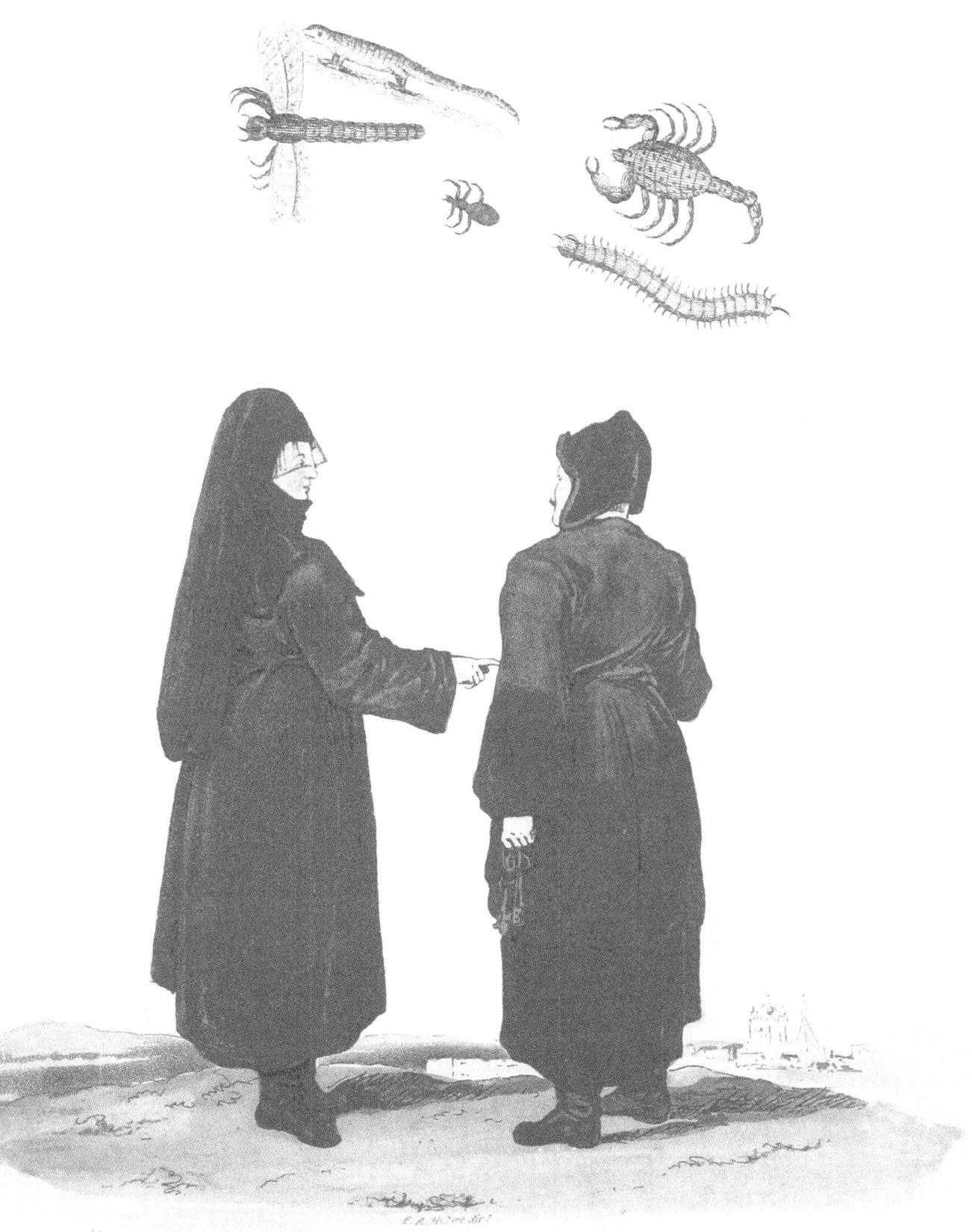

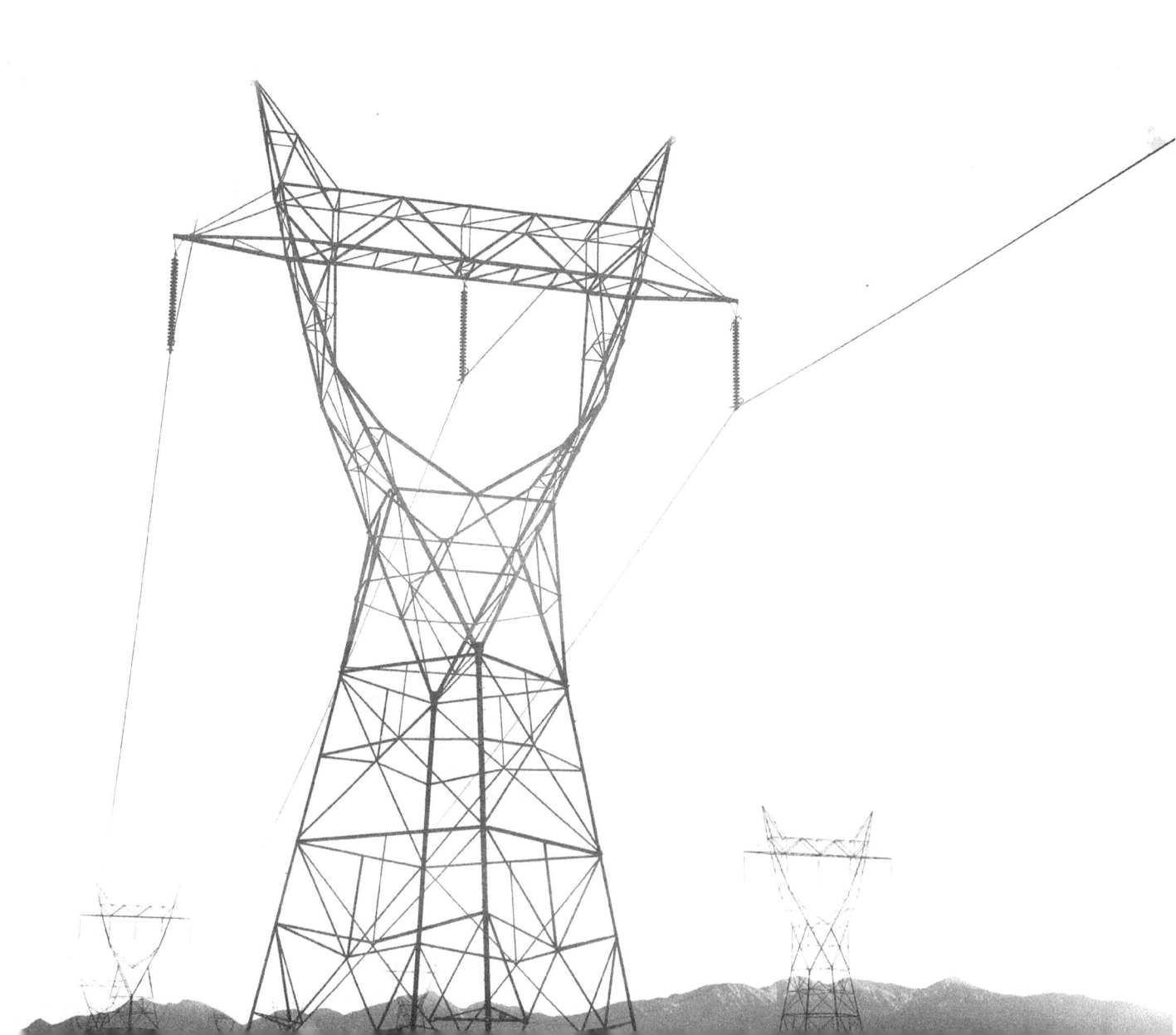

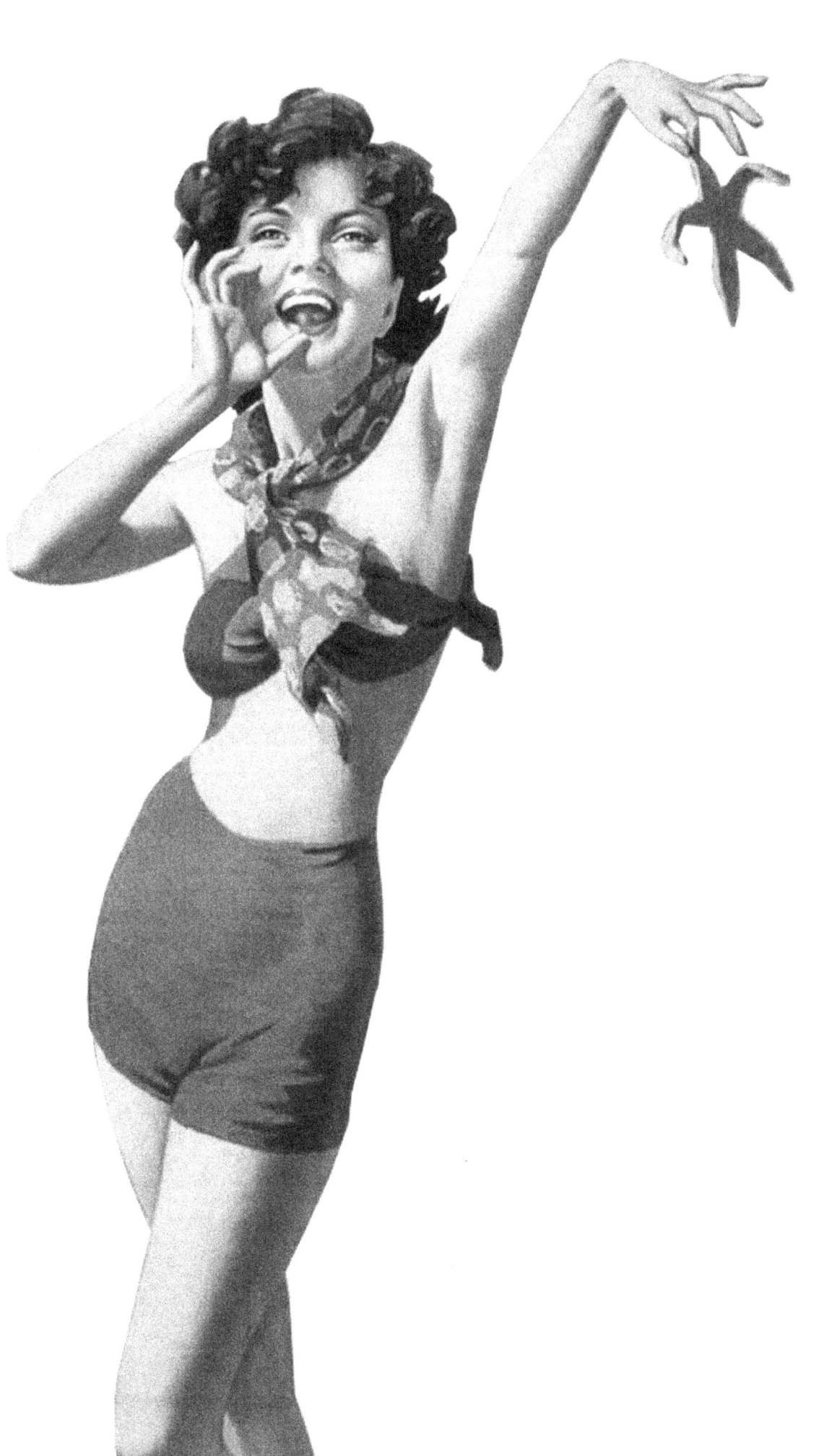

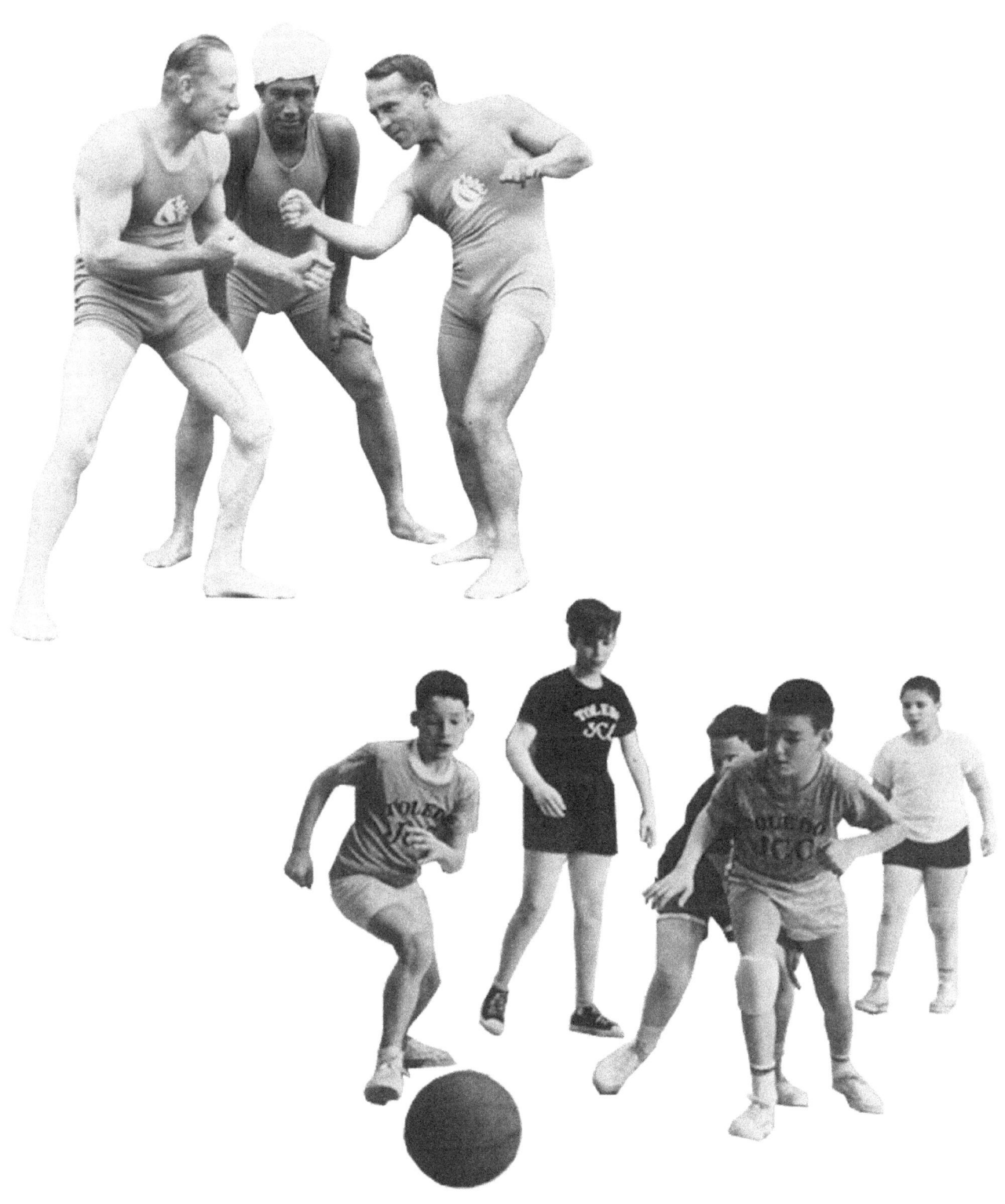

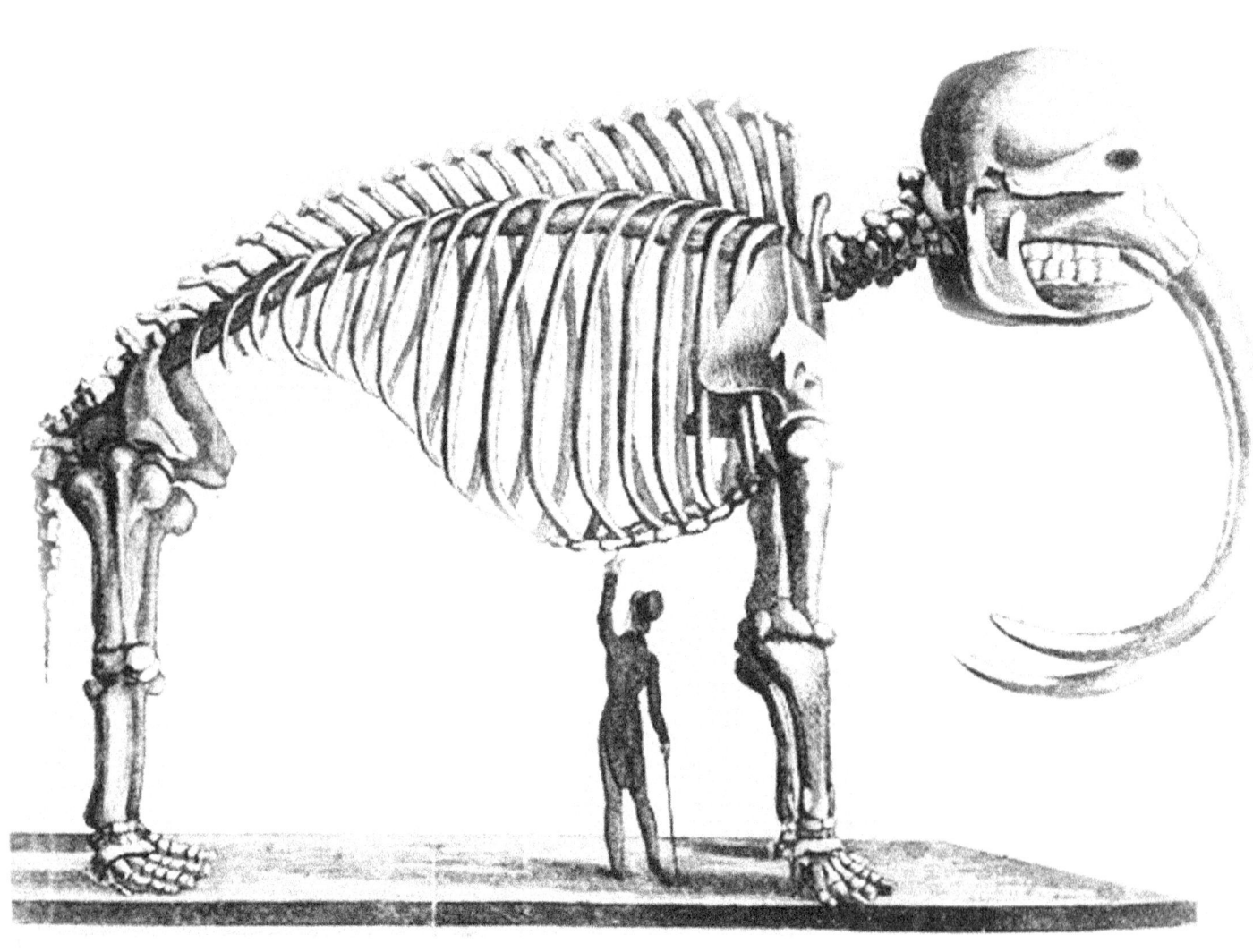

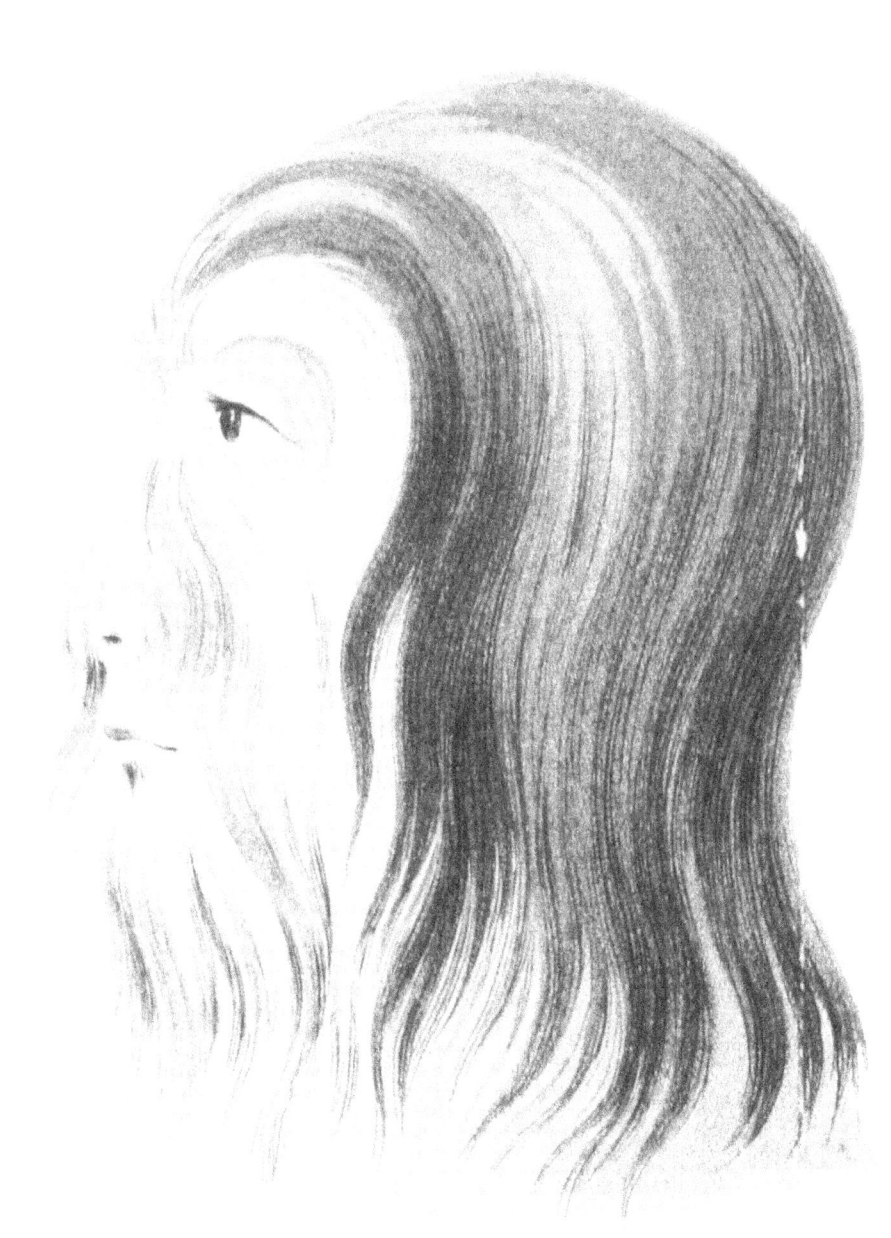

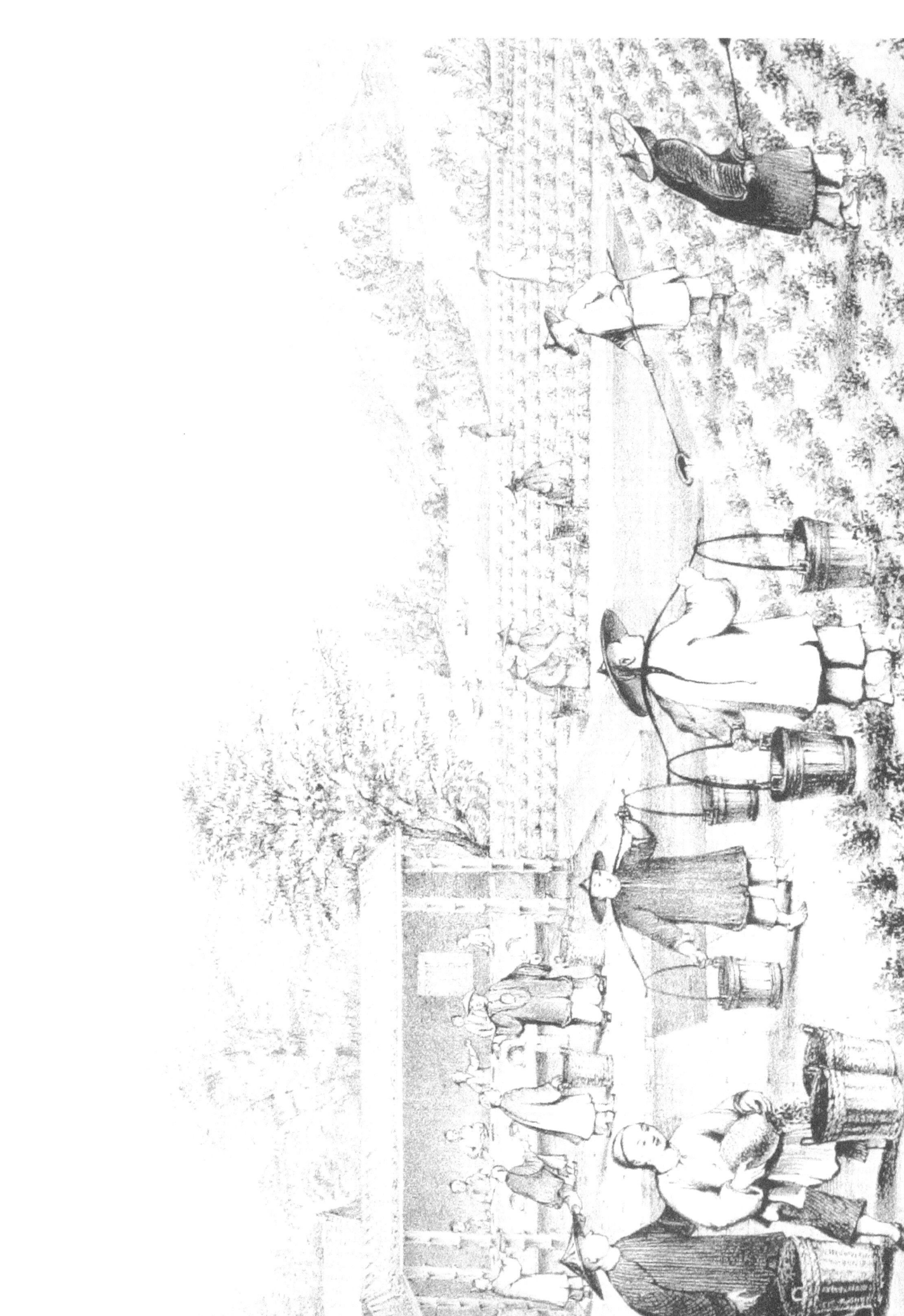

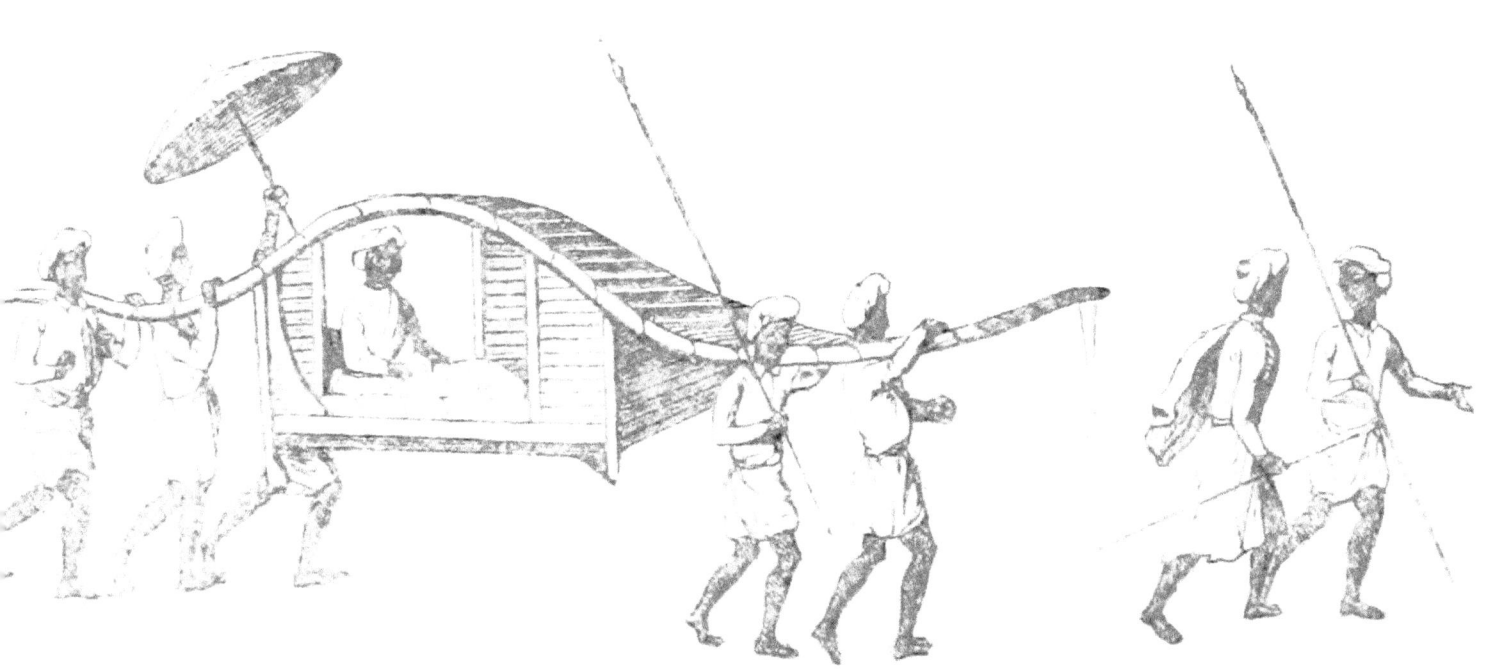

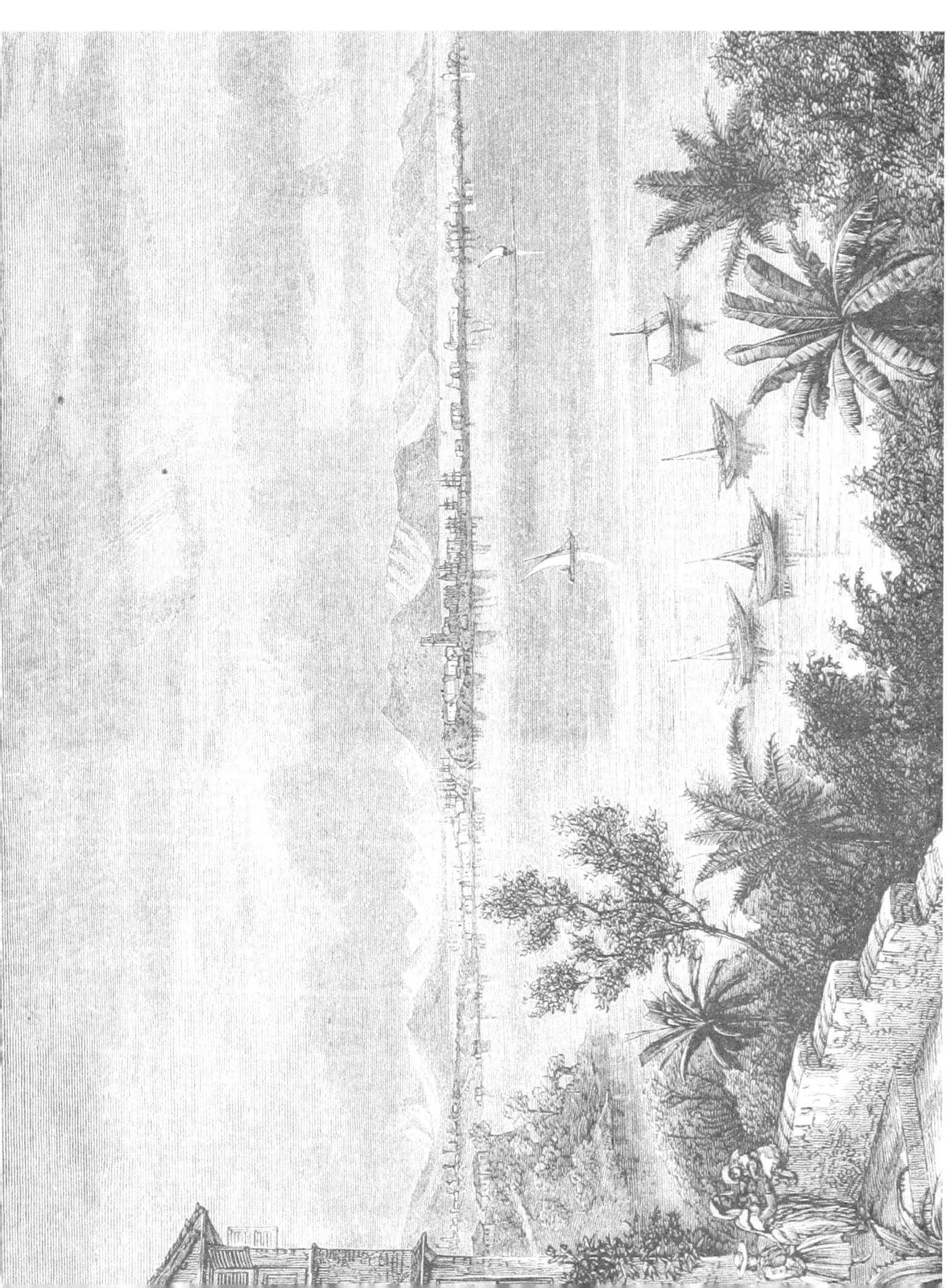

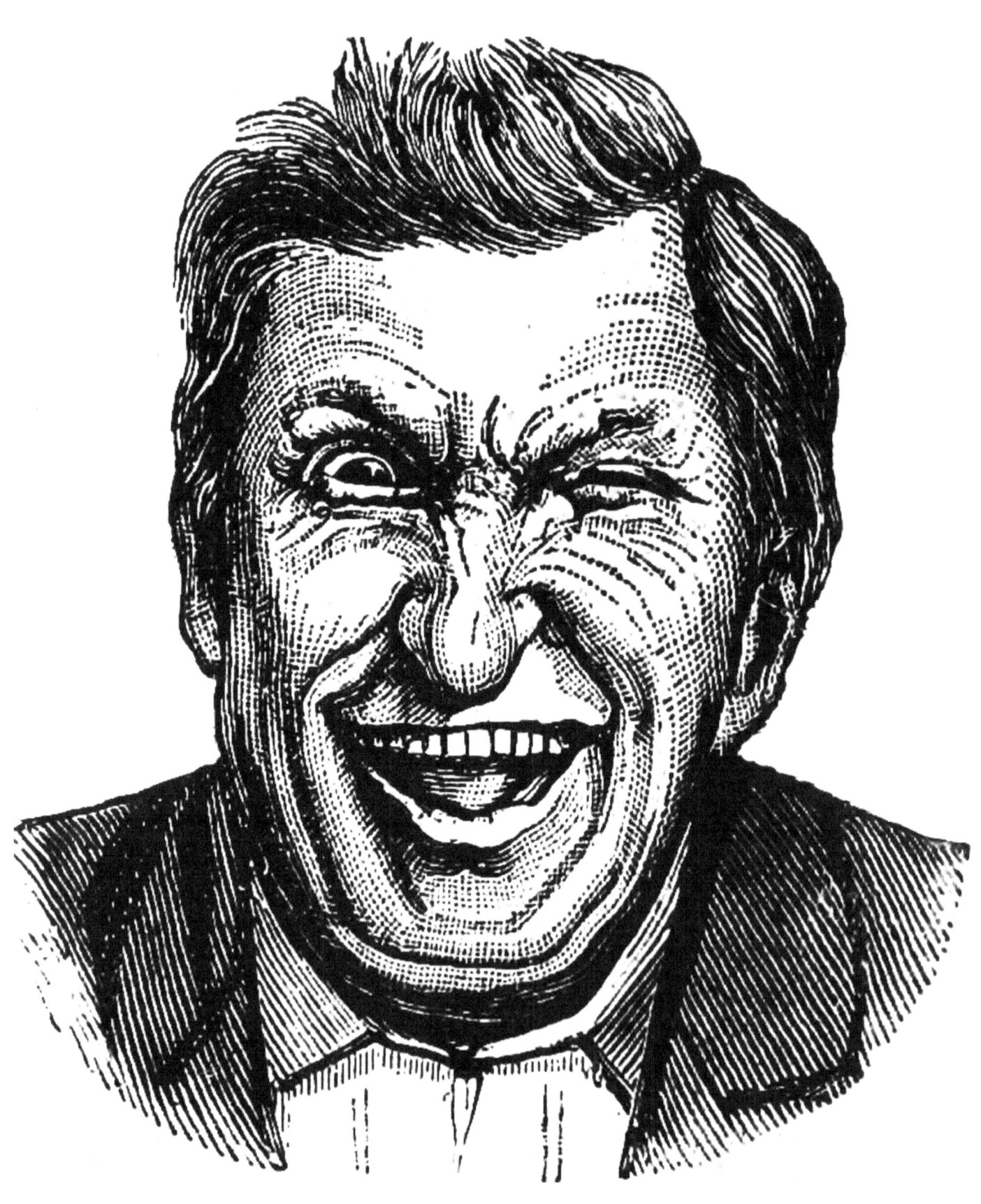

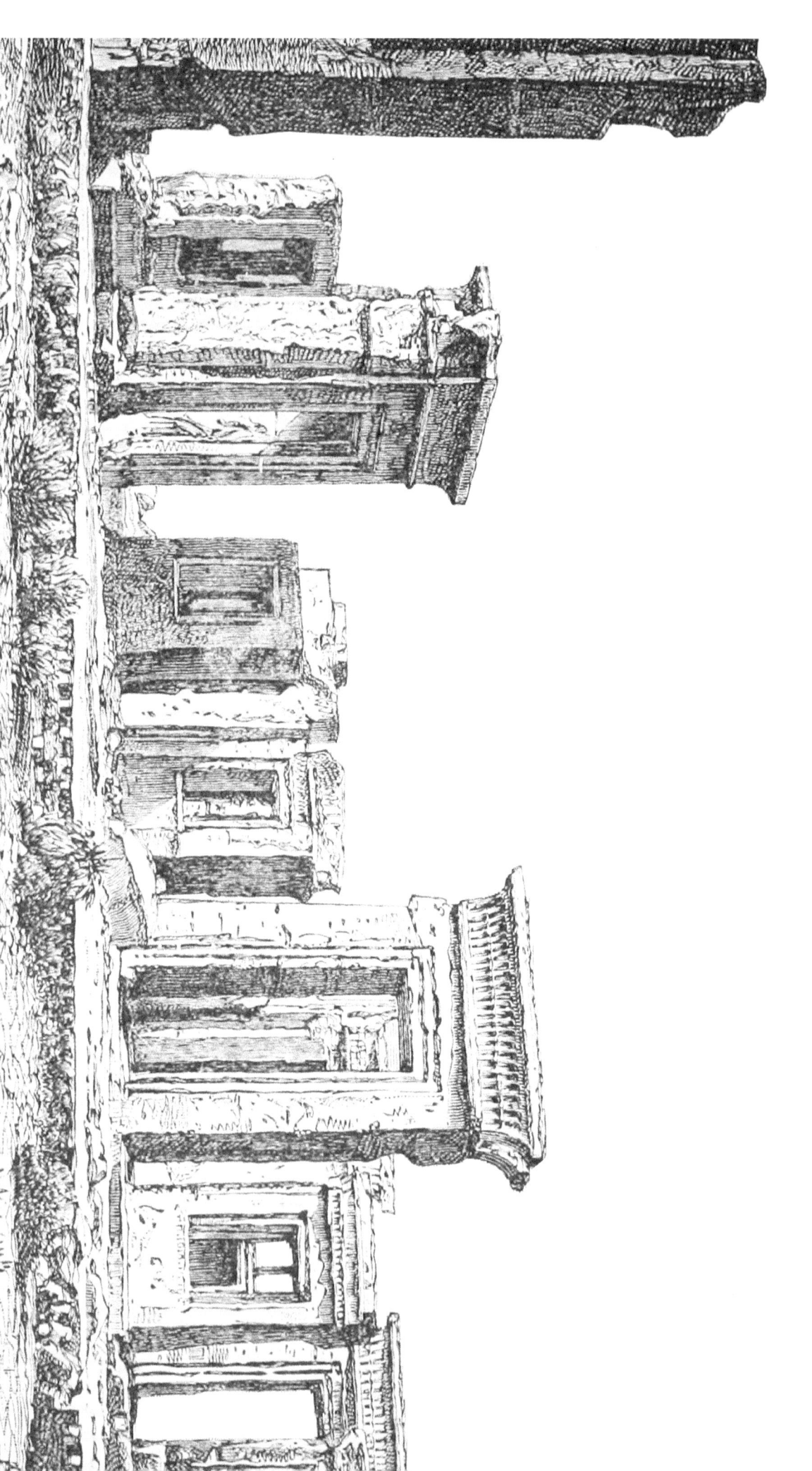

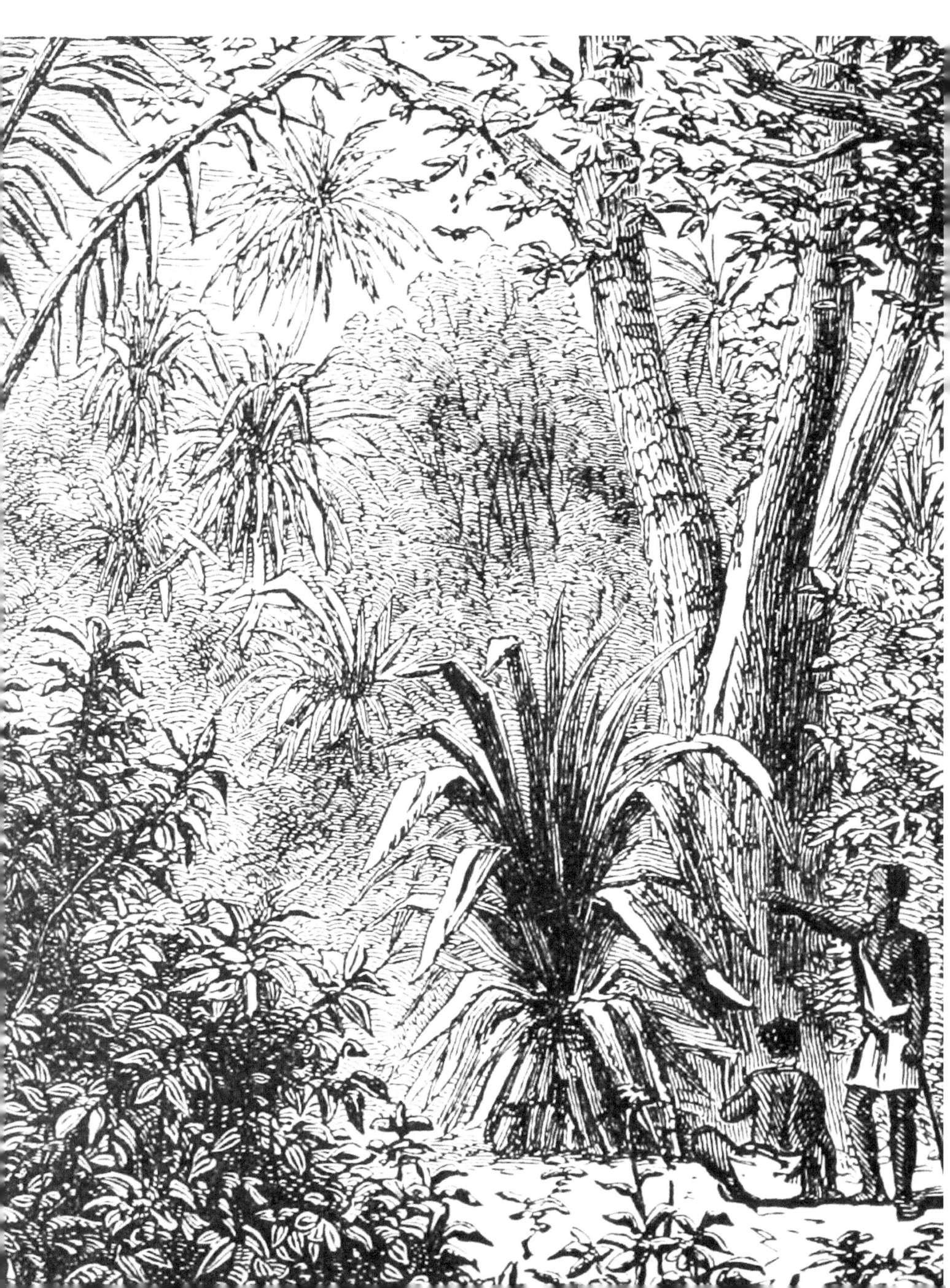

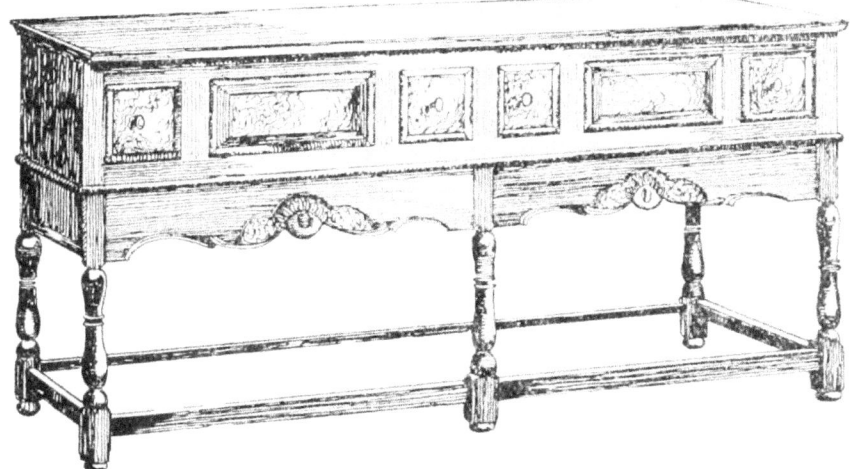

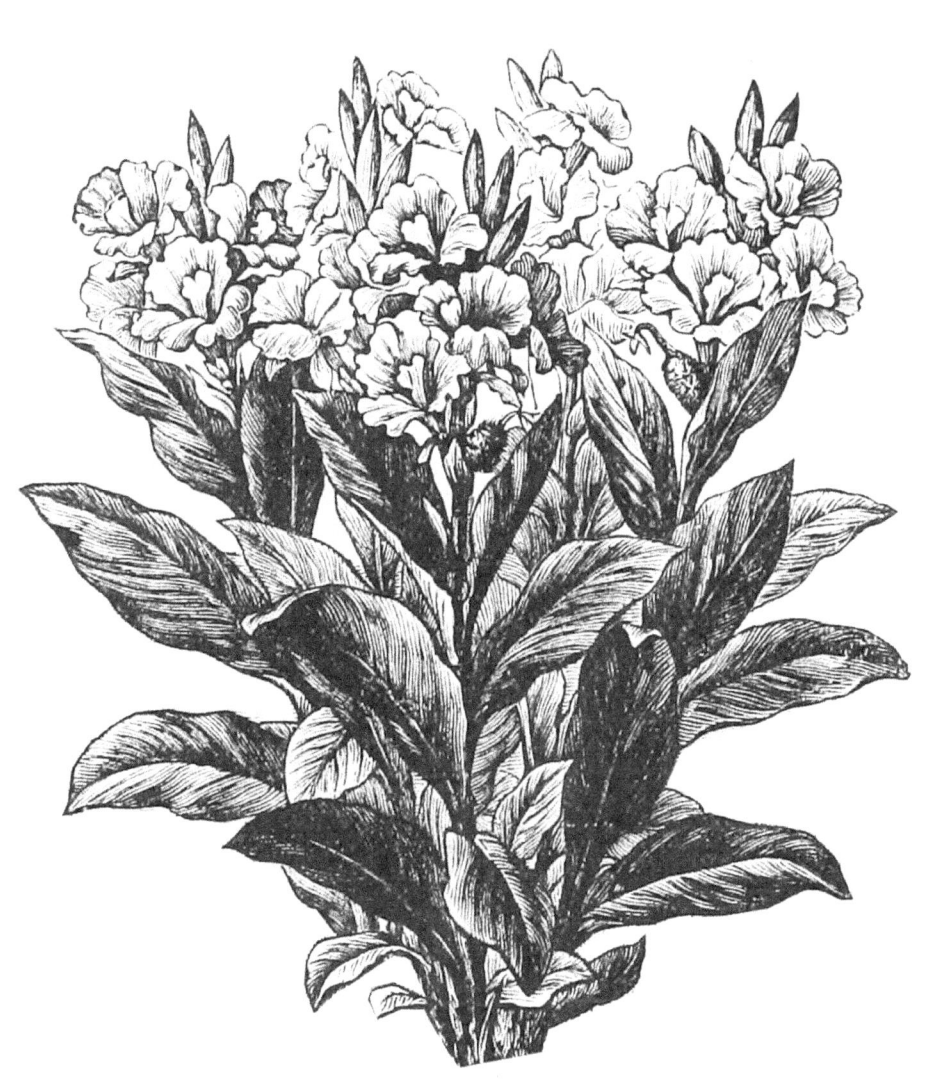

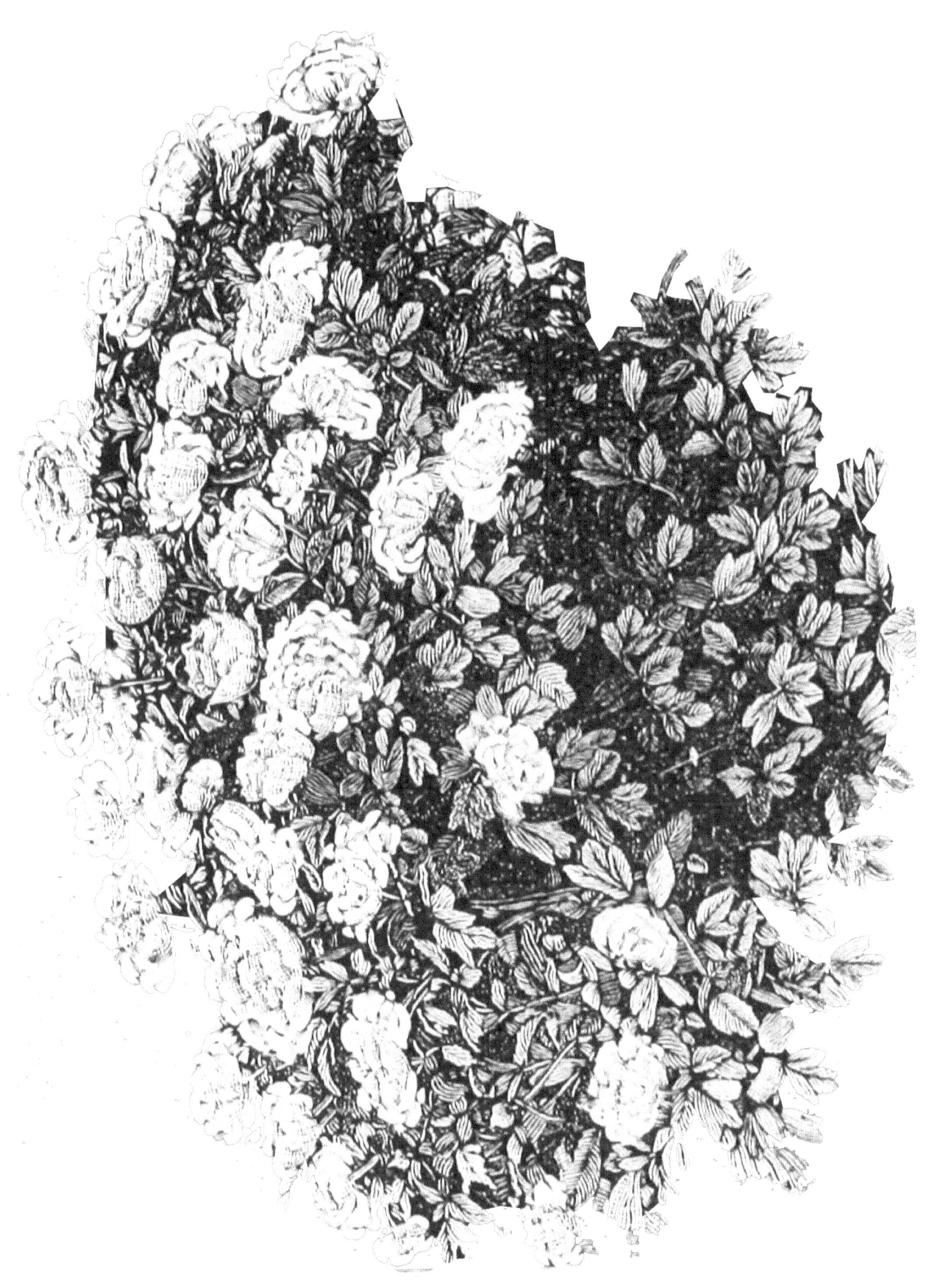

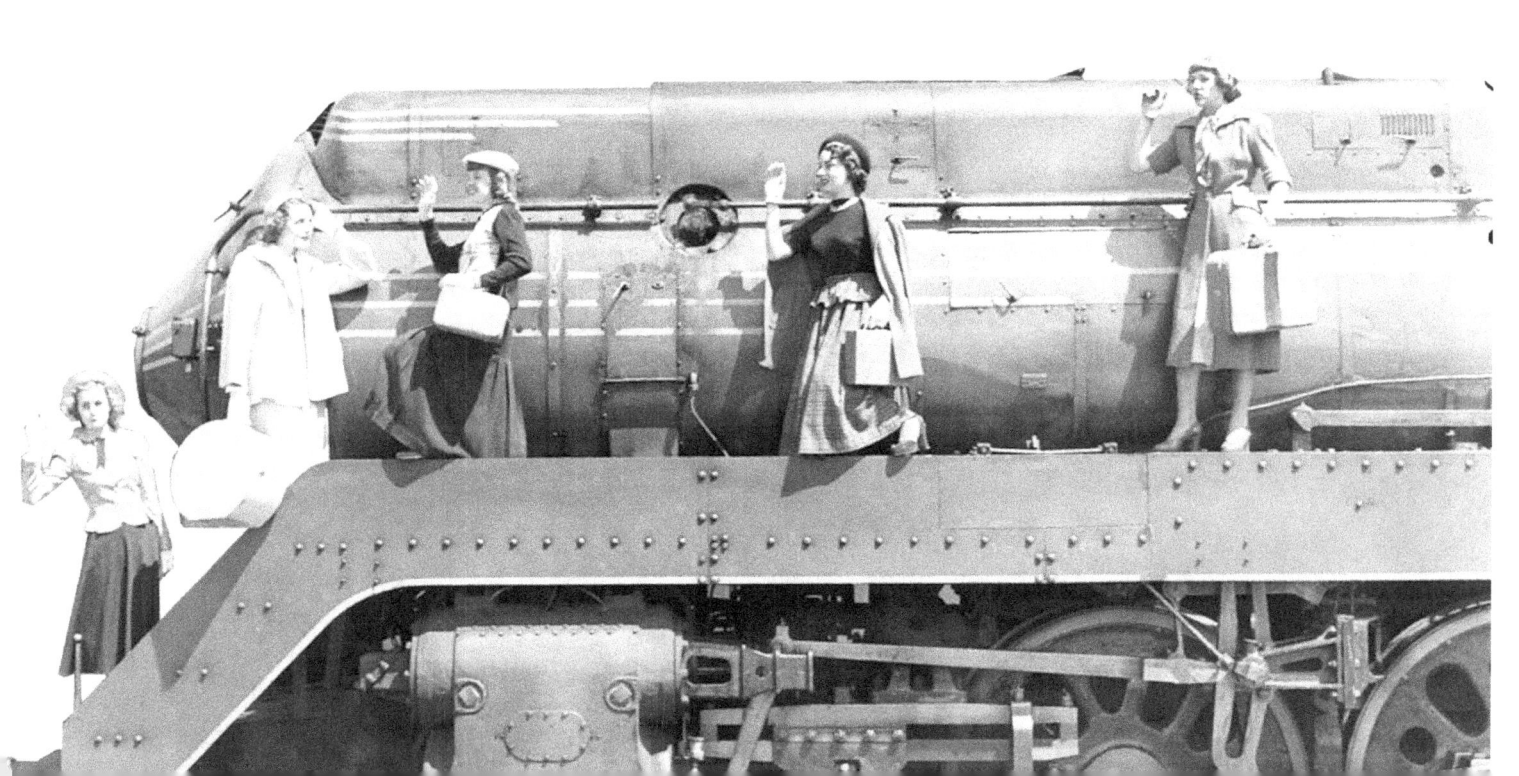

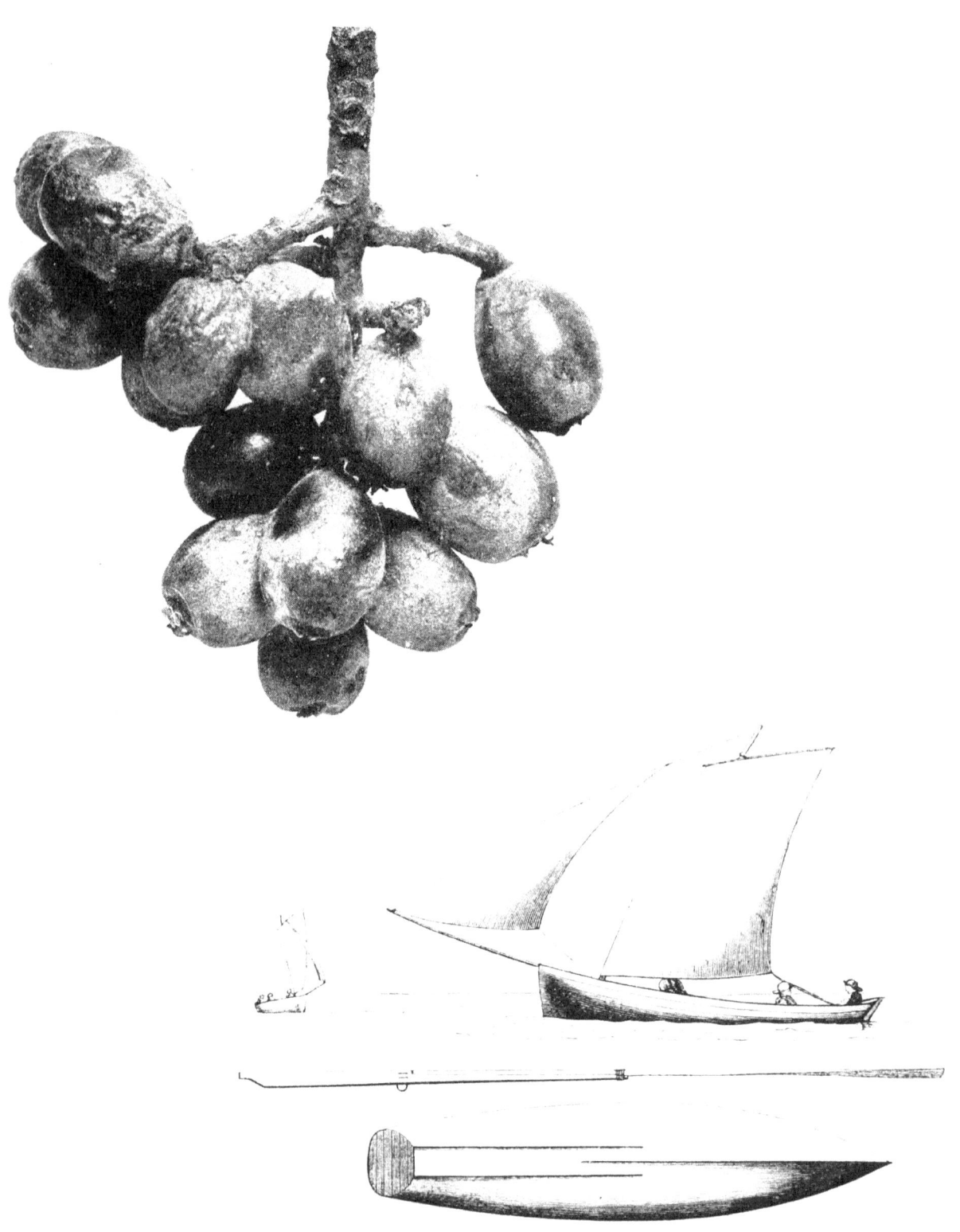

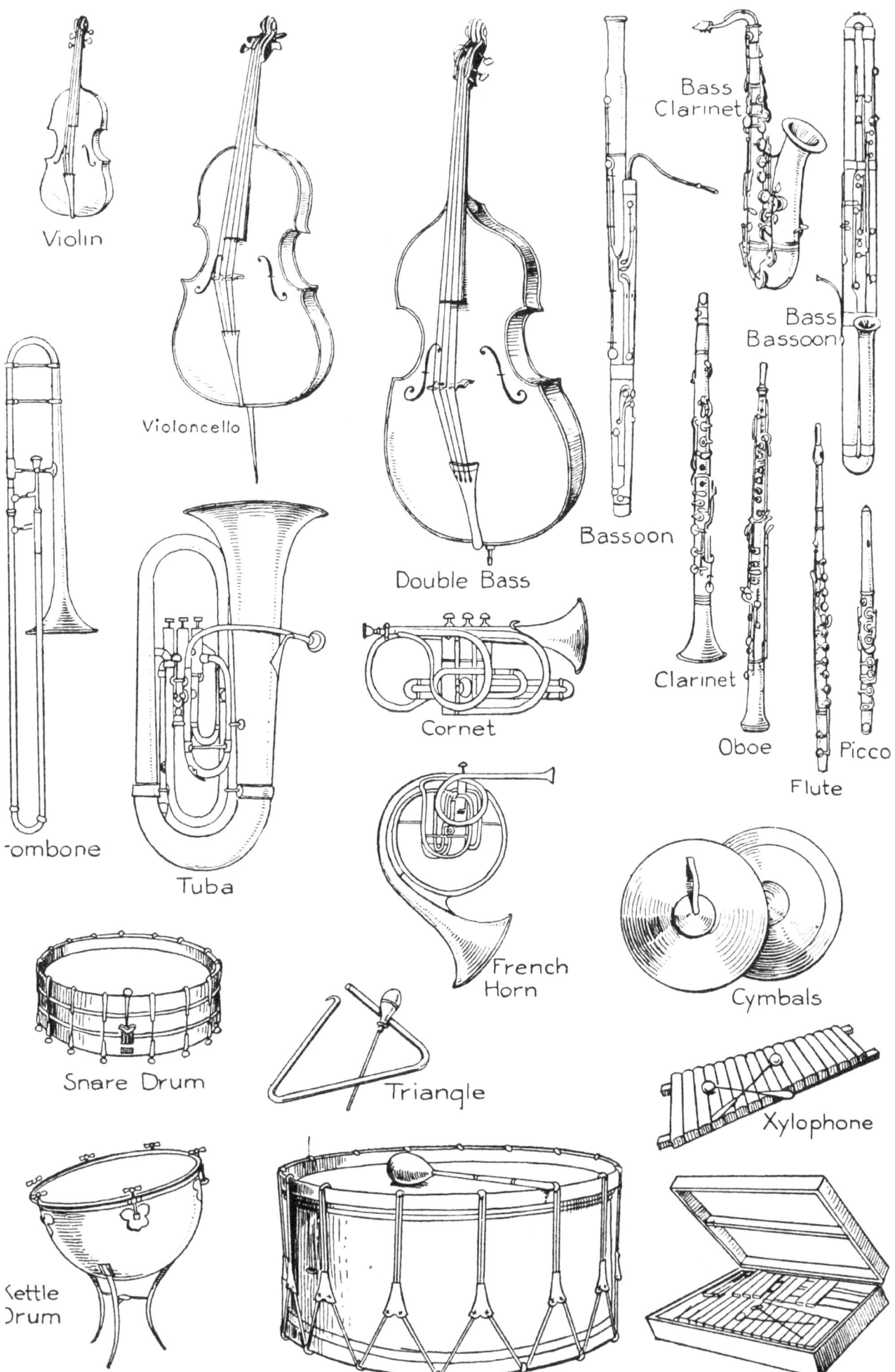

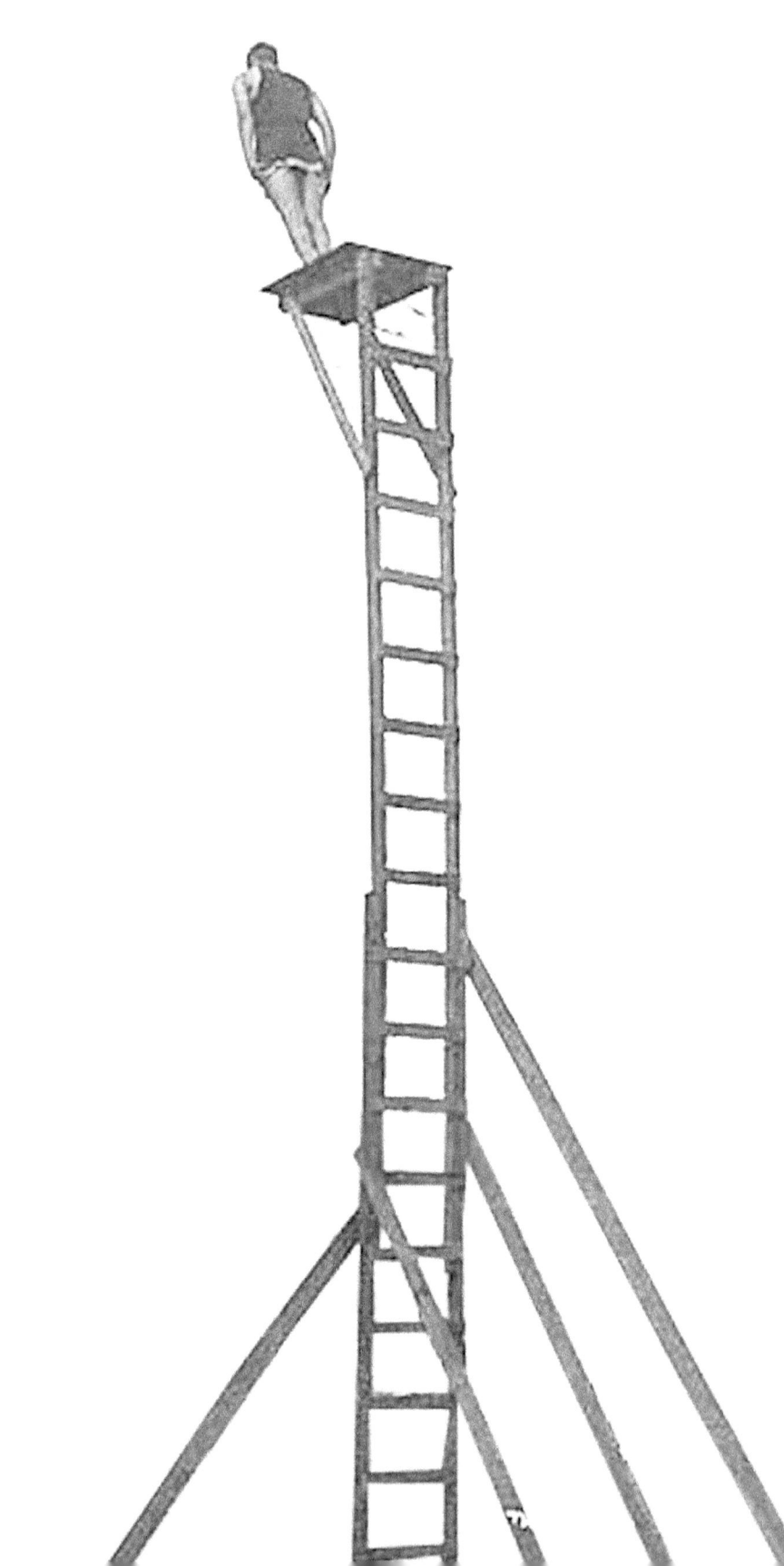

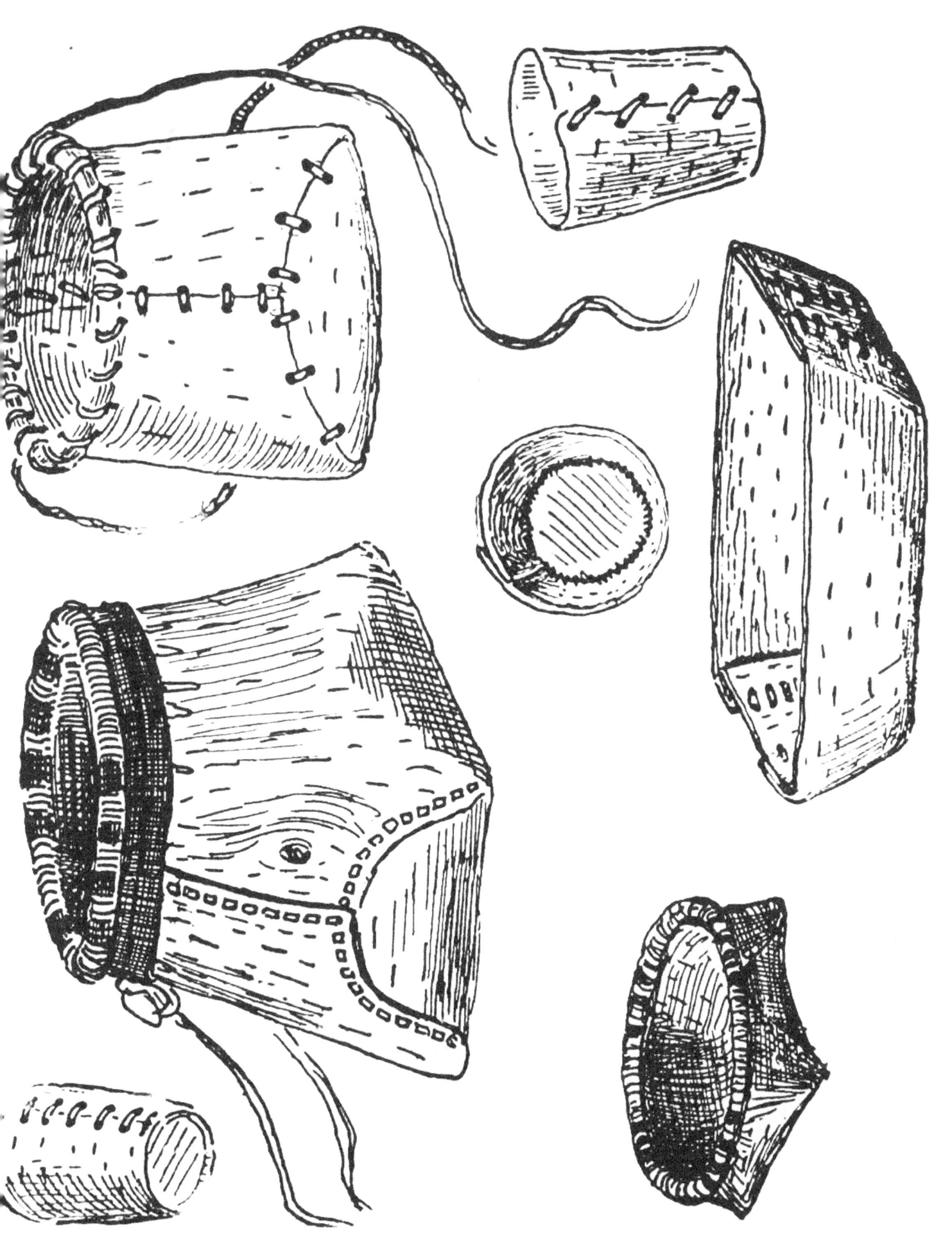

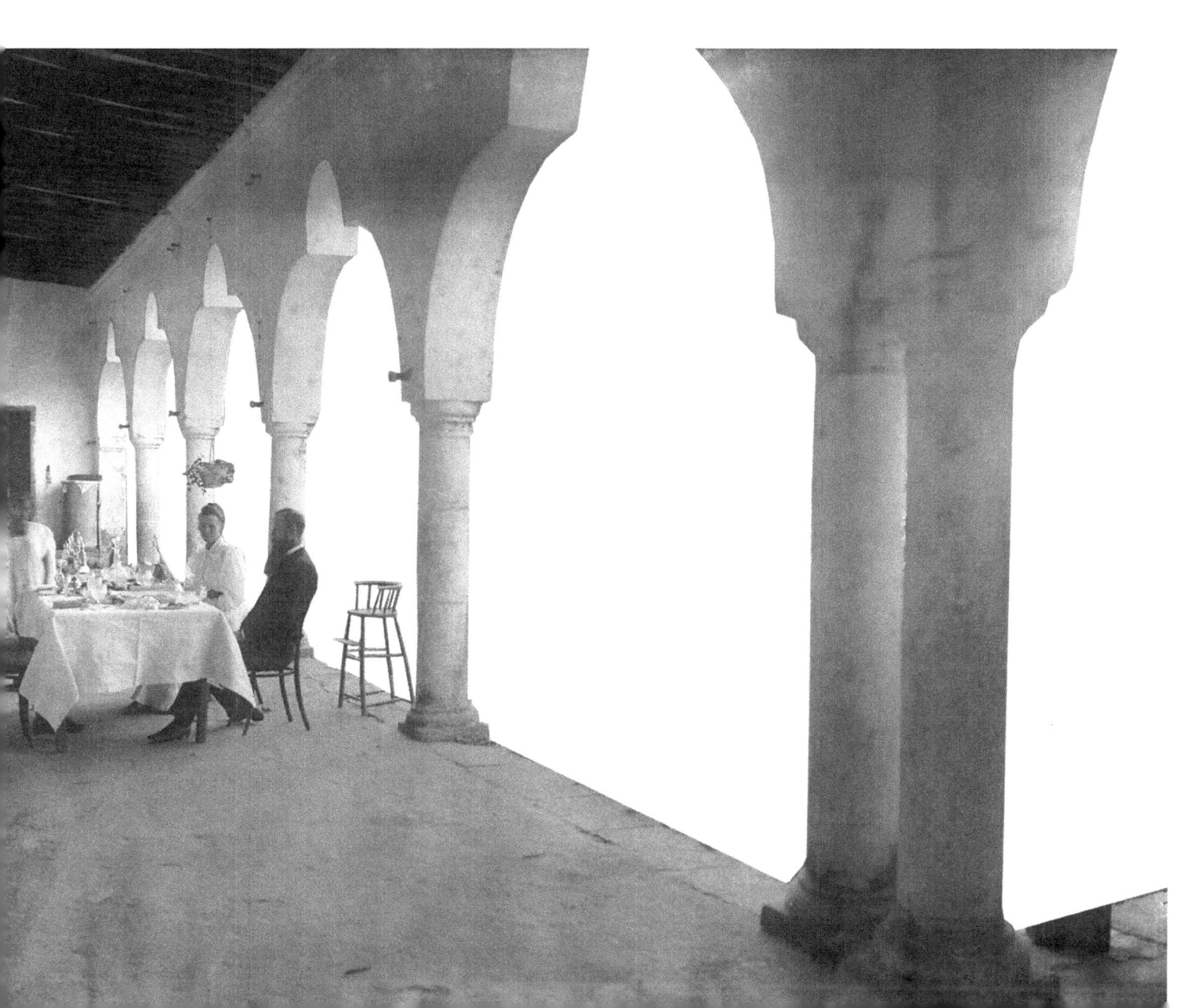

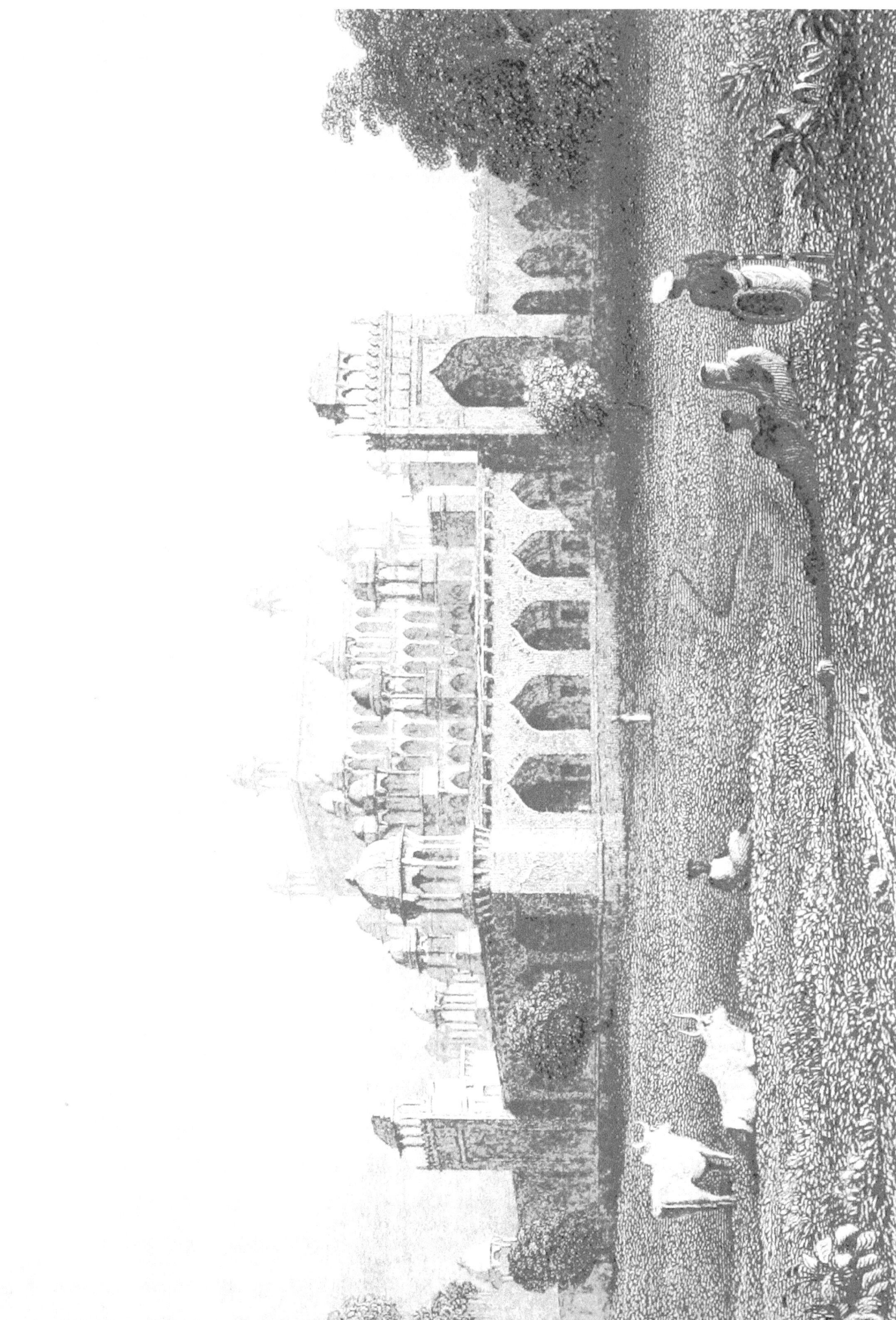

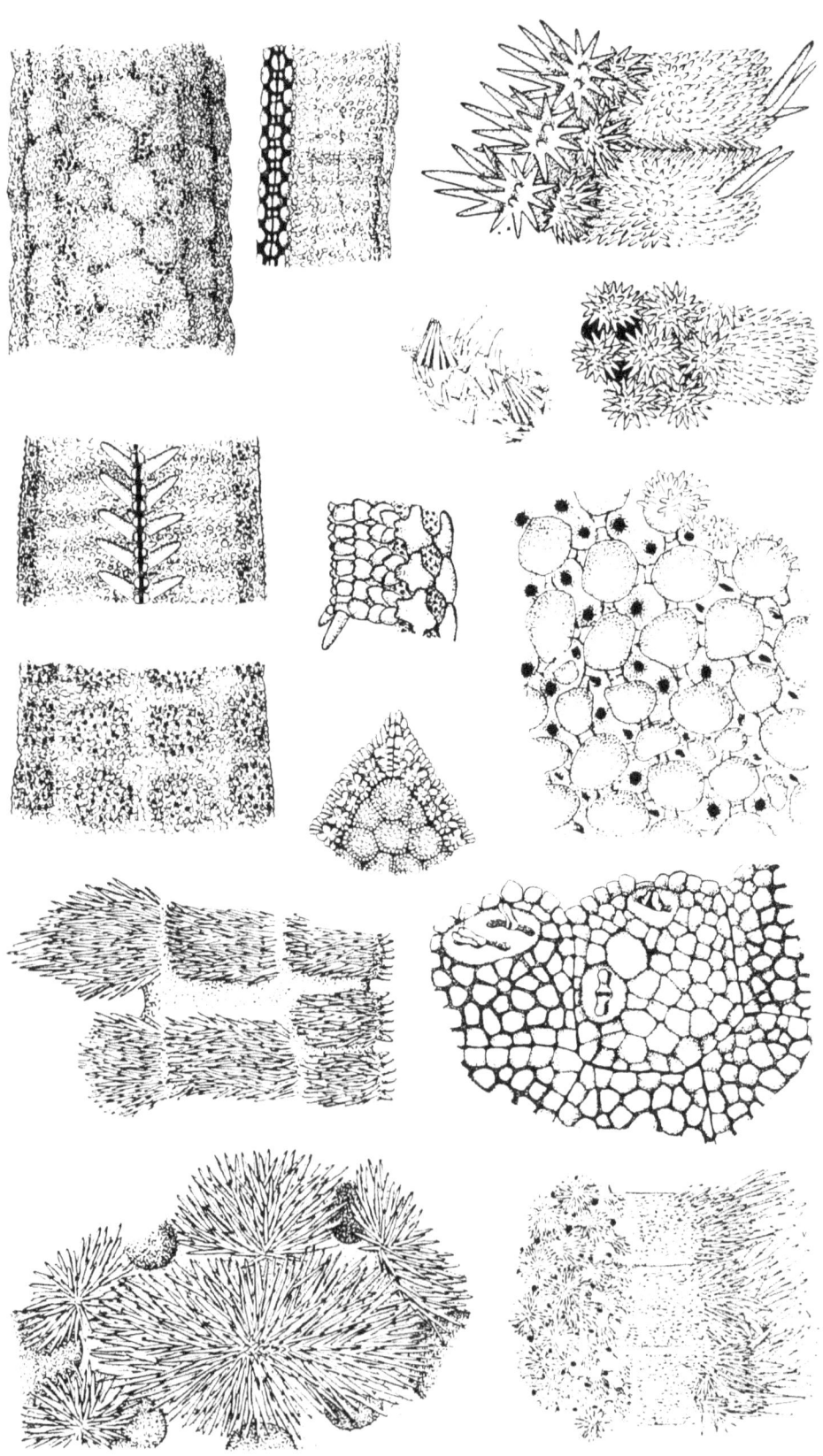

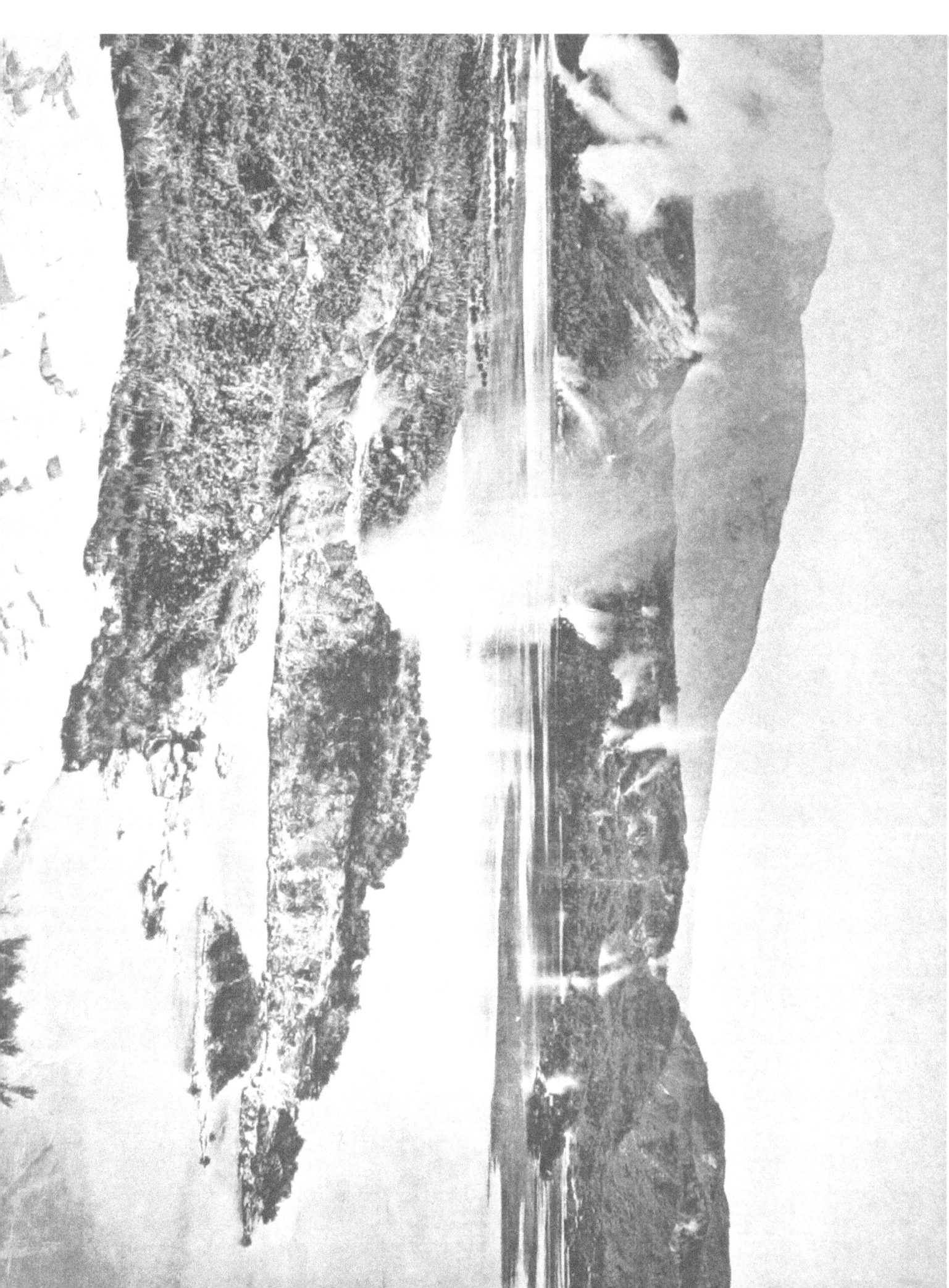

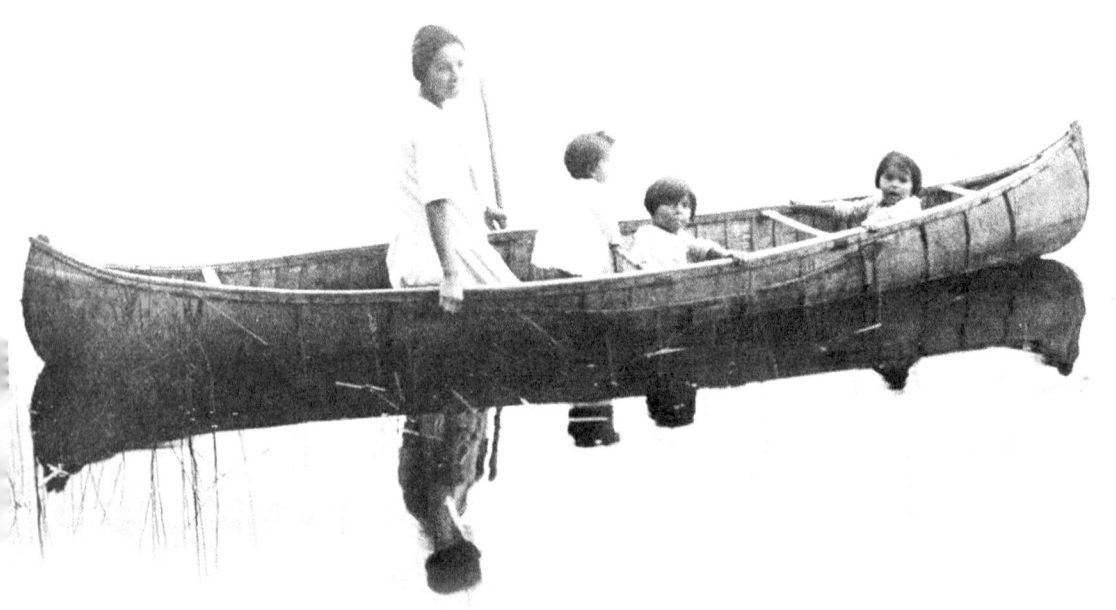

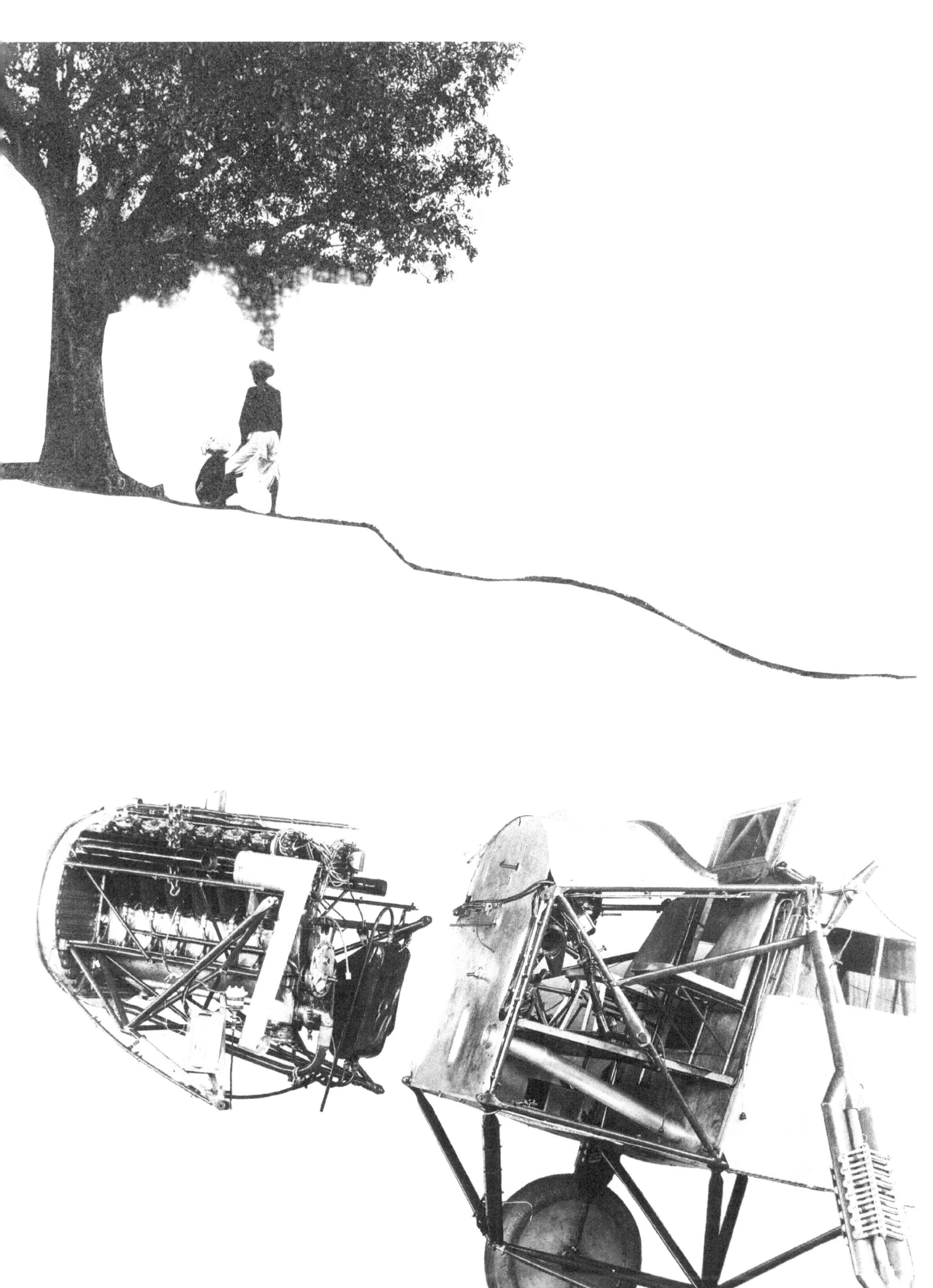

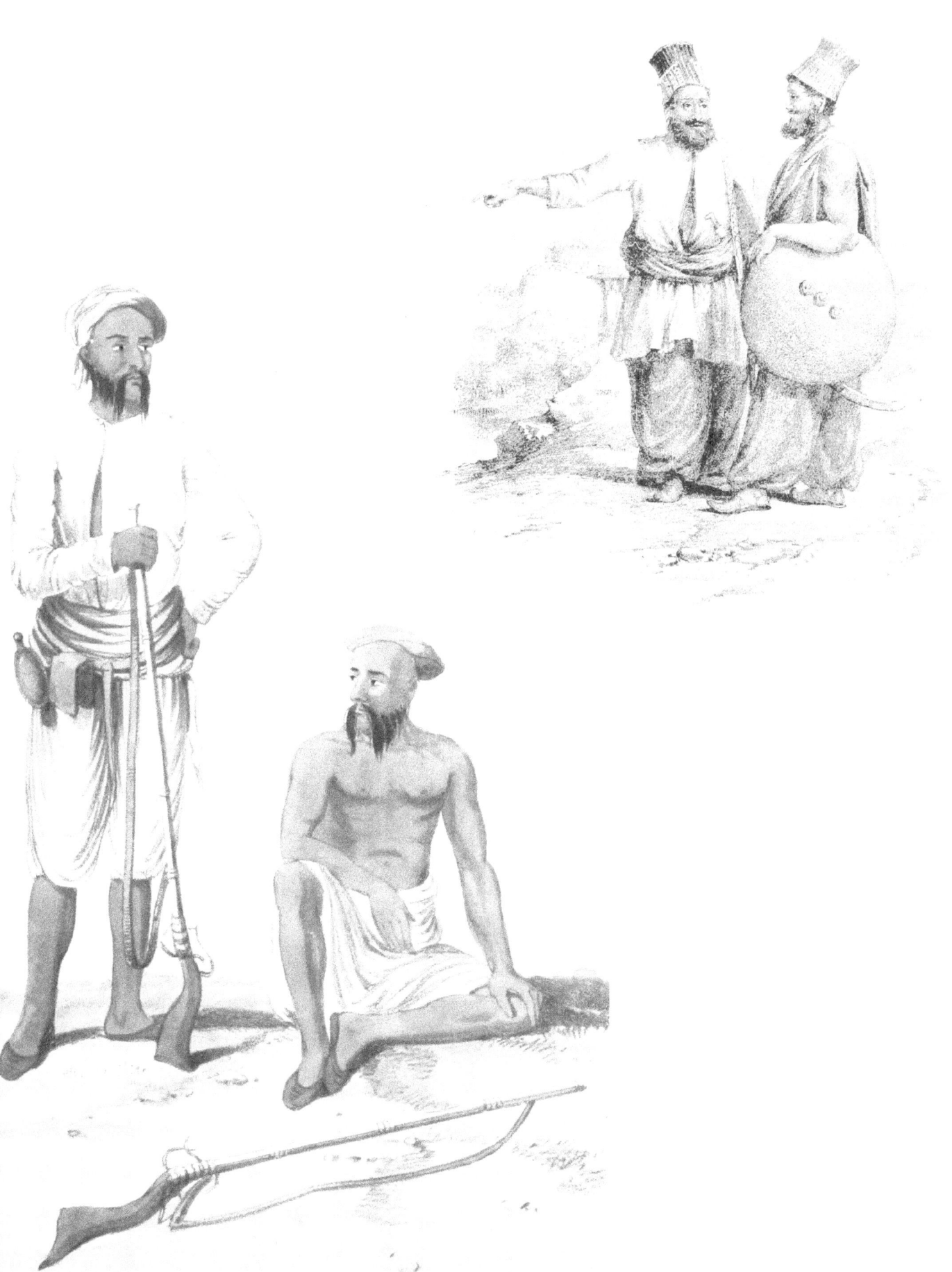

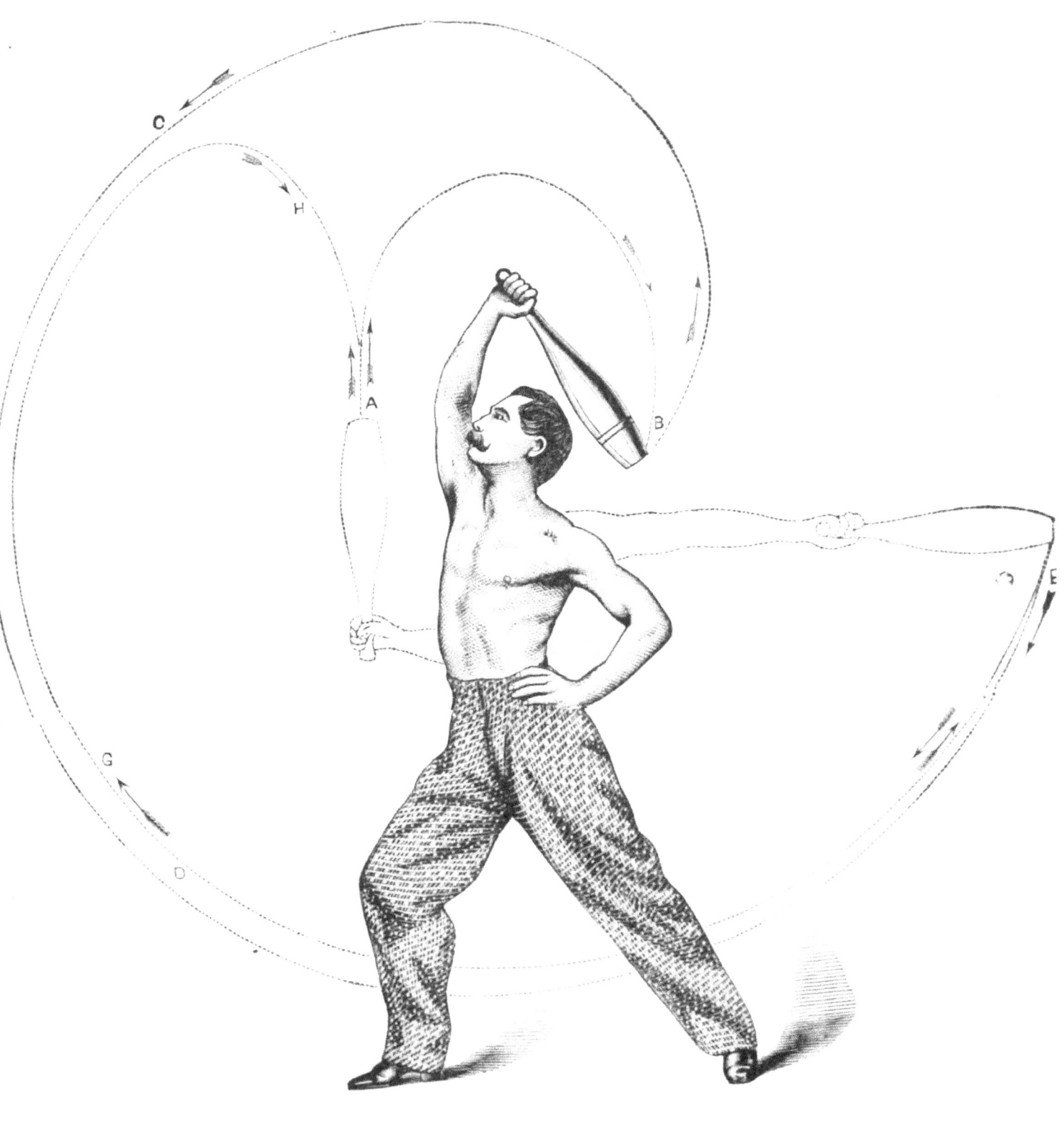

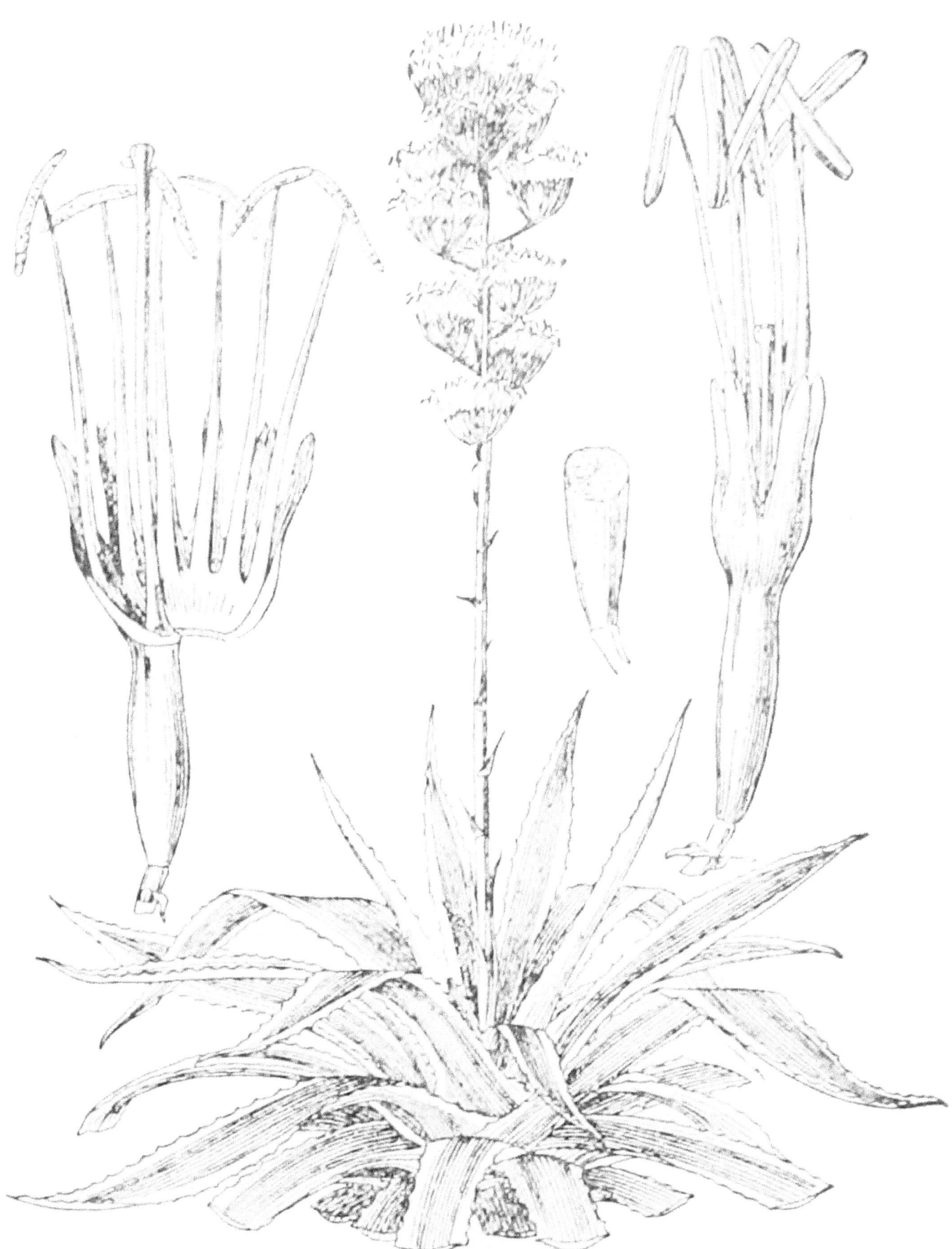

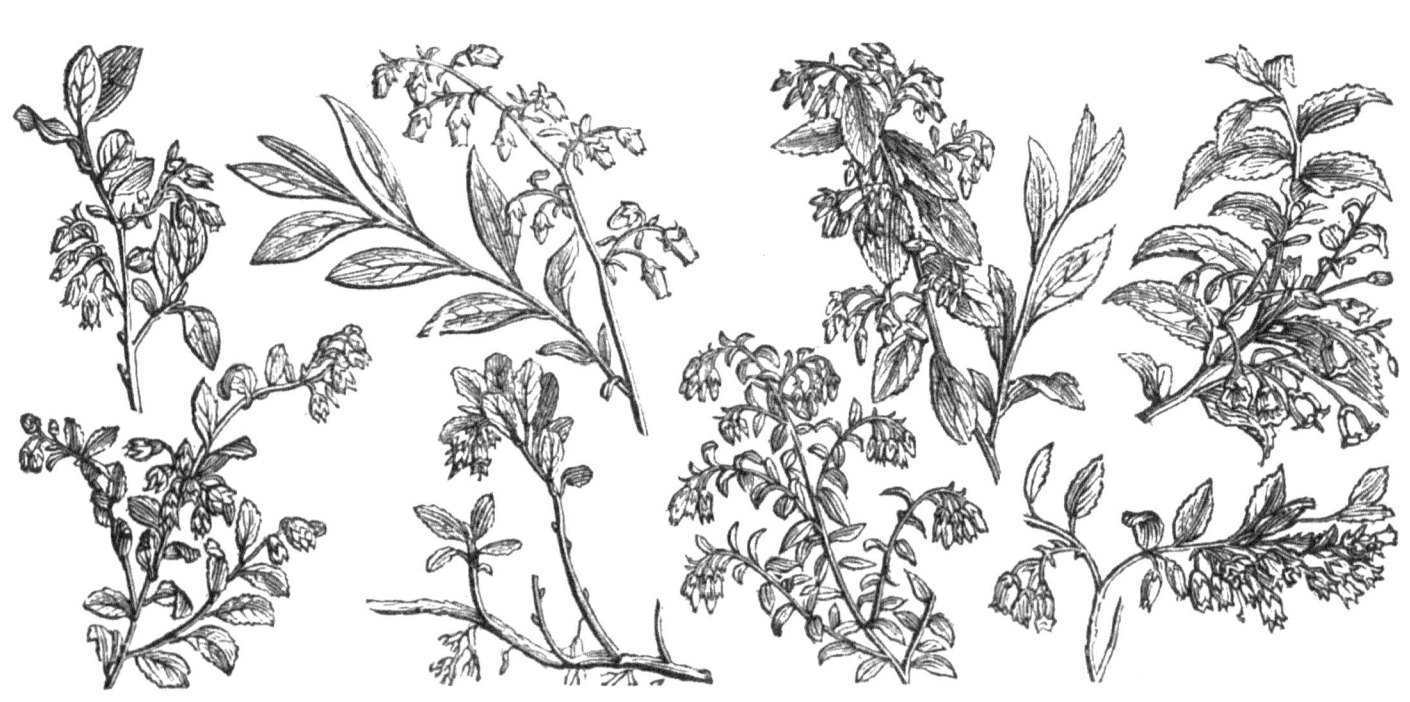

www.ingramcontent.com/pod-product-compliance
Lightning Source LLC
Chambersburg PA
CBHW082250220526
45469CB00009B/2941